LUDWIG'S HANDBOOK

of New Testament Rulers & Cities

CHARLES LUDWIG

ACCENT BOOKS
Denver, Colorado 80215

ACCENT BOOKS

A division of Accent Publications, Inc.
12100 W. Sixth Avenue
P. O. Box 15337
Denver, Colorado 80215

First published in 1976 as *Cities in New Testament Times* and *Rulers of New
Testament Times*, this work has been updated and combined into one volume
for clarity and convenience.

Library of Congress Catalog Card Number 83-71619
ISBN 0-89636-111-X

First Printing 1983
Second Printing 1984

Credits

The author wishes to express thanks to the following publishers for granting permission to quote from their works.

E.P. Dutton, New York, for Pliny's Letter to Trajan, from *Private Letters, Pagan and Christian*, by Dorothy Brooke. Copyright by E. P. Dutton, Inc.; renewal 1958 by Lady Dorothy Brooke.

Penguin Books Ltd., London, for quotations from *The History of the Church from Christ to Constantine* (pages 111, 161, 162), translated by G. A. Williamson. Copyrighted 1965 by G. A. Williamson. Republished by Penguin Classics, 1965.

Simon and Schuster, New York for quotations from *Caesar and Christ* by Will Durant. Copyright 1944 by Will Durant.

A. P. Watt and Son, London, for quotations from *The Twelve Caesars* by Suetonius, translated by Robert Graves and published by Penguin Classics. Permission granted by Robert Graves. Copyright 1957.

Contents

Preface

The man behind the projector was embarrassed.

His trip to Israel had been one of the most exciting experiences of his life. But now as he was showing the slides he had taken to his friends, he was unable to identify many of them. "This one I think was taken in Jericho—No, that isn't right— Oh, I know now, it was taken in Bethlehem—If only Marj were here! She kept a diary. . . . "

As he spoke, a hollow place formed in his stomach.

It was a painful evening and everyone was glad when the lights were turned on. Unfortunately, this was not an isolated case. The solution to such tragedies is extremely simple. *Travelers should read about the sites before they get to them*! And that is one of the purposes of this book.

Another purpose of the book is to make the New Testament come to life for the ordinary reader. One of the great scenes in the New Testament is when Jesus stood as a prisoner before Herod Antipas. This was God in the hands of a man! Ah, but the drama increases for the reader when he learns that this Herod was the son of the Herod who tried to kill the infant

Jesus. And the drama gets a further nudge when we realize that this Herod had also had trouble with the Sanhedrin. Indeed, he had had so much trouble with that august body, he had ordered forty-five of them put to death.

Or let us take a look at Paul as he stood bound before Felix. Here, again, the drama tightens when we learn that Felix was a former slave; and that even during the trial he was in such trouble with the Roman Government he feared for his life.

To many, such places as Tarsus, Ephesus, and Antioch are just vague names with no real meaning. But if such people could visualize an eager messenger carrying an epistle along the Via Egnatia; or if they could think of Cleopatra, dressed like Aphrodite, sailing up the Cydnus to Tarsus, those cities would leap into life and demand to be studied.

The rulers and the cities and the events of the early Christian times were extremely interesting. This book will help lift them out of the forgotten past into present reality.

Formerly, this work was published as two books: *Rulers of New Testament Times*, and *Cities in New Testament Times*. In this larger volume new material has been added as well as valuable information provided the reader in the the two appendixes.

Charles Ludwig
Tucson, Arizona

Chapter 1

Augustus, the Teen-Age Emperor

Crammed within his triangular skull was more ability than that posessed by a handful of ordinary men. According to historians, he stands shoulder to shoulder with Constantine the Great as one of the Empire's most creative rulers. They called him Augustus Caesar. But strangely, Augustus was not his real name; and although Rome knew her greatest glory under him, he started his flamboyant career when he was an awkward teenager of eighteen!

In describing the birth of Christ, Luke wrote: "And it came to pass in those days, that there went out a decree from Caesar Augustus, that all the world should be taxed" (Luke 2:1). By that simple statement, he pinpointed the date; for all civilization knew about Augustus Caesar!

Augustus Caesar, the first emperor of the Roman Empire, was one of the most colorful men who ever lived. But since at the time Augustus came to power in 27 B.C., Rome had been in existence for more than half a millennium, we wonder how he could have been the "first emperor."

The answer is simple. It lies in the *form* of government that had been, and the new form that came into being under Augustus.

AUGUSTUS

As early as 509 B.C.—the year the Roman Republic was founded—Rome had started to grope for a democratic form of government. This early republic came into being after the disposal of the shadowy, almost mythical, Tarquinius Superbus, the last of the Roman kings.

This early republic was a crude form of democracy. Voting was limited to men, and they had to be citizens. Also, their votes were limited to Yes or No—and could only be cast at meetings summoned by a consul or tribune! Suggested amendments were not allowed. Moreover, voters were partitioned into units known as *centuries*, for they were made up of one hundred men.

The number of centuries was strictly controlled by either class or wealth. Citizens were divided into two main groups, *patricians* and *plebeians*. The patricians, descendants of important families, were considered full citizens; while the plebeians had a limited citizenship.

Patricians and business men were allowed eighteen centuries; "First Class men"—those with 100,000 asses' worth of property—were allowed eighty centuries; those with 75,000 asses' worth had less. And the number kept decreasing until those who had less than 11,000 asses' worth of property had to be content with a mere thirty centuries. (An *ass* in 1942 was equivalent to about six American cents. In 1982, 100,000 asses might be worth around $30,000.)

With this system, decisions favoring the rich and upper classes were guaranteed.

Across the centuries, the Roman republican system varied. In 494 B.C. the plebeians persuaded the patricians to grant them an assembly. But their assembly didn't gain legal power until 287 B.C.—more than two centuries later!

In 60 B.C., three prominent leaders—Pompey, Crassus, and Julius Caesar—formed the First Triumvirate in the republic. This was a dictatorship of three men. They worked together in an attempt to restore order to Rome and her colonies in a fading republic. Crassus was killed fighting the Parthians in 53

B.C., and Pompey and Caesar soon quarreled. Caesar defeated Pompey in 48 and became sole dictator in 46 B.C.

Caesar began work on a far-reaching program that included many of the reforms proposed in the Senate during the previous century. Caesar, however, was murdered in 44 B.C. As he was dying from the wounds he received in the Roman Senate, those who witnessed his assassination wondered who his successor would be. Mark Antony was all but certain that he was the chosen one.

But on the 19th of March, when he secured the will from the Vestal Virgins—a bevy of girls who had vowed to remain pure, and whose main task was to guard the sacred fire burning at the hearth for the national goddess, Vesta—he was stunned to learn that Caesar had bequeathed his fortune to his three grandnephews, and that he had named one of them—Caius Octavius—his son and heir!

Antony—known for his gross immorality—had already summoned Caesar's army to Rome. Alarmed by the famous general's power, the Senate hastened to invite young Caius Octavius to Rome. At the time the message arrived, Caius was with the army at Apollonia in Illyria. The lad was shocked at the news of his great-uncle's death. He and Julius had been very close. They had traveled to Spain together, and during the last several years Caius had spent much of his time in the palace at Rome.

As Caius Octavius approached the city on the Tiber, his mother advised him to stay in hiding—warning that Antony would kill him. But although Caius was only eighteen, he was no coward. He went to see Antony and had a heart-to-heart talk with him.

To the boy's horror, he found that Antony was not obeying Julius Caesar's will. Instead, he was raising an army to subdue Brutus who had refused to give up his claim on Cisalpine Gaul. The will had bequeathed three hundred sesterces (a little over one hundred dollars) to every Roman citizen. When Caius suggested that this should be paid, Antony managed one delay after another. Caius then borrowed the money and paid the legacy to each of Caesar's veterans. Next, he changed his name to Caius Julius Caesar Octavianus and proceeded to raise an army of his own.

Soon the armies met at Mutina—in north central Italy. There was a sharp fight and Octavian's forces won. Octavian then returned to Rome in triumph. Next a compromise was arranged. The Senate voted for a Second Triumverate. Octavian became the ruler of the West; Antony was given Egypt, Greece, and the East; and Lepidus was put in charge of Africa.

But before the three Triumvirs settled down to govern, they decided to eliminate their enemies and confiscate their property. A long list was drawn up. This sinister document included three hundred senators and two thousand businessmen. The entire list was condemned to death without trial.

"To have money became a capital crime; children to whom fortunes had been left were condemned and killed; widows were shorn of their legacies; 1400 rich women were required to turn over a large share of their property to the Triumvirs; at last even the savings deposited with the Vestal Virgins were seized. . . . The Triumvirs set soldiers to guard all exits from the city. The proscribed hid in wells, sewers, attics, chimneys. . . . Salvius the tribune, knowing himself doomed, gave a last feast to his friends; the emissaries of the Triumvirs entered, cut off his head, left his body at the the table, and bade the feast go on. Slaves took the opportunity to get rid of hard masters, but many fought to death to protect their owners; one disguised himself as his master and suffered decapitation in his stead. . . .

"By Antony's command Cicero's right hand was . . . cut off and brought with the head to the Triumvir. Antony laughed in triumph, gave the assassins 250,000 drachmas, and had head and hand hung up in the Forum." (*Caesar and Christ* by Will Durant.)

At the end of the bloodbath, the Triumvirs combined their armies and marched through Macedonia and Thrace where they sought a confrontation with the forces of Brutus and Cassius—the assassins of Julius Caesar.

But even as the Triumvirs marched, Cassius and Brutus were busy strengthening their armies. In desperate need of funds to pay their troops, they forced the cities in the Eastern Empire to pay their taxes ten years in advance. Cassius sent his soldiers to Tarsus, where Paul was to be born some years later. He placed them in the homes of the citizens and vowed that they would not leave until what is equal to $9,000,000 had been raised. And in order to obtain this money, municipal lands were sold at auction; boys and girls and later older people were made into slaves; and the temple vessels were melted down for their precious metal.

Cassius also went into Judea. There, he demanded an amount equal to $4,200,000. And since the cash was not available, he sold the entire population of four towns into slavery.

Finally, in September 42 B.C., the rival armies met on the plains just below Philippi—the city where the jailer was converted. The Triumvirs were successful; and Cassius asked his shield-bearer to kill him and the man obeyed. Brutus, also, took his own life by throwing himself on his sword.

One would think that this would be the end of the fighting. Not so; for now Antony and Octavian faced each other. Antony had married Octavian's sister and had lived with her until he fell for the charms of Cleopatra and began to have children by her.

The dispute between these brothers-in-law came to a flaming end on September 2, 31 B.C., when the two met in a gigantic sea battle at Actium—just off the western coast of Greece. Octavian's men managed to set fire to Antony and Cleopatra's ships. An ancient writer described the holocaust. "Some sailors perished by the smoke before the flames reached them; others were roasted in their vessels as though in ovens. Many

13

leaped into the sea. . . . "

Between them, Antony and Cleopatra had 500 ships. Nonetheless, they lost and fled. Later, they both committed suicide—he, by thrusting a dagger into himself, and she, by allowing an asp to bite her breast.

Octavian was now master of the world and the Mediterranean had become a Roman lake. He even controlled the Roman colonies in Africa for Lepidus had retired. With his new power, Octavian proceeded to put the Empire in order. He stopped piracy which had been running wild, punished corrupt officials, and established a firm government of law and order. While doing this, he raided the treasury of Egypt and brought the money to Rome. This provided such an overabundance of money that interest rates fell from twelve to four percent and the value of real estate soared.

Next, he reorganized the government and had himself named *princeps senatus* which roughly means "first on the roll call of the Senate."

With his firm hand, money came out of hiding and an abundant prosperity settled over the entire Empire. The Senate was so thankful for his success they gave him the title *Augustus*. The title comes from the word *augere* which means to increase. Formerly it was used only in connection with holy objects.

What kind of man was this Augustus who ruled so serenely while Jesus was spending His youthful years in Nazareth? History informs us that he had sandy hair, merging brows, an odd-shaped head, and penetrating eyes. He suffered from a kind of ringworm that caused his skin to itch; had gallstones; and was so sensitive to the cold that in winter he wore "a woolen chest protector, wraps for his thighs and shins, an undershirt, four tunics (blouses), and a heavy toga"(Will Durant).

Also, a form of rheumatism had so crippled his left leg he walked with a slight limp. He could not ride horseback long, tired easily, and his right hand frequently became stiff with what might have been arthritis. These and other problems made him a near-invalid. But he managed to survive, for he was scrupulously careful with his diet. He insisted on only the plainest foods. A typical meal consisted of a little fish, cheese, coarse bread, and fruit. Often he ate alone—especially before a banquet. Thus he had an excuse not to eat the rich foods that were being served.

Usually he treated his illnesses with home remedies; but when a doctor cured him of a serious disease, he was so thankful he decreed that all doctors in the Empire were exempt from taxation! One wonders if this ruling was still in effect in the days of Luke the physician.

Augustus was superstitious. He carried a sealskin to protect himself from lightning and he was very careful about his activities during "unlucky" days. Modesty, he believed, was a virtue. He lived in a gaudy age. Still, he refused to succomb to its lure. He wore clothes woven by the women of the palace and insisted on sleeping in a tiny room dubbed the *cubiculum*.

About the time Jesus was being taken by His parents to the Temple in Jerusalem, a revolt against Roman authority was organized in Germany. The Roman governor Varus was lured into a trap beyond the Rhine and he along with three legions were utterly destroyed. When Augustus was informed of the disaster, he was so shaken he refused to shave or cut his hair for months. And sometimes he repeatedly dashed his head against the wall while he wailed: "Quintilius Varus, give me back my legions!"

Oddly enough, one of Rome's problems was that of a lowering birthrate among its citizens. Large families became decidedly unpopular and so the practice of infanticide became widespread. Infants were left out in the cold to perish. At the same time people were freeing their slaves because they were too poor to feed them; and since the state supplied free food to all freedmen, the state had to look after them. In addition, many slaves were buying their freedom.

Augustus became alarmed over the situation. He feared that the racial stock of Rome was changing. In order to stop this, he had a series of unique laws passed. One of these decreed that the owner of two slaves might free both of them; but the owner of from three to ten slaves could only free half of them; and no one was allowed to free more than one hundred slaves.

Also, he tried to encourage Romans to have more children. A lady worth more than 20,000 sesterces was required to pay a one percent tax on her wealth each year. But this tax was reduced on the birth of each child, and after the third child it was eliminated completely. Augustus denounced racial suicide and made lavish gifts to many who raised large families. When a slave had quintuplets, he had a monument raised in her honor.

Augustus was horrified at the lowering of the moral standard, even though his own morals were extremely questionable. He decreed that teenagers could not go to public entertainments unless they were accompanied by an adult relative. Women were not allowed at athletic contests, and were restricted to the upper seats at gladiatorial fights.

The emperor who started to rule the Empire as a teenager continued to rule until his death in A.D. 14. At that time he was seventy-six. His life overflowed with crime; but he had a steady hand. Without knowing it, he helped make way for the spread of Christianity. He did this by strengthening the postal system, establishing a vast network of roads, and by keeping a relative peace throughout the world.

As he was dying, he quoted the last lines from a Roman comedy: "Since well I've played my part, clap now your hands, and with applause dismiss me from the stage." He then embraced his third wife, Livia; bade her farewell, and was gone.

His body was cremated on the Field of Mars.

Chapter 2

Mama's Boy, Tiberius Caesar

Some called him "Mud-and-Blood"; others "The Old Goat." And when he died many Romans were so relieved they risked their lives by shouting: "To the Tiber with Tiberius!" Nevertheless, this mama's boy ruled the Roman Empire from A.D. 14-37. And since this rule, like a shadow, extended across the ministry of John the Baptist, the resurrection of Jesus Christ, and the conversion of Paul, the story of Tiberius Caesar is extremely important.

Indeed, the fact that Christianity could be born and flower with such a monster on the throne, is one of the proofs of the vitality of the gospel!

When the disciples handled coins with the image of Tiberius on them, they saw a tall, broad-shouldered man with fine, deep-set eyes. Tiberius wore his hair low over the nape of his neck, and he was so strong he could "poke a finger through a sound, newly-plucked apple" declared Suetonius. And yet he was shy and miserable because of acne!

Few killed others with as little reason as Tiberius. Thousands were executed during his reign. He signed death warrants with the same carelessness with which he ate his

17

food. And yet he was so dominated by his mother he allowed her to co-sign many of his imperial decrees!

Tiberius was the first of the Julio-Claudian dynasty which ended with the Nero who executed Paul. Historians believe he became emperor only through chance, and a slight one at that. At the time of the birth of Jesus, Augustus Caesar was on the throne. Soon the roving eye of Augustus fell on Livia, the wife of a former admiral of Julius Caesar's fleet. At the time, Livia had already borne one child to her husband and another was on the way. Such trivialities, however, did not matter to the great Augustus. He insisted that she marry him immediately; and this she did even though it so crushed her husband he died shortly afterwards.

Livia's first child was Tiberius and thus Augustus became his stepfather. Tiberius had the most aristocratic blood in Italy. Both parents were Claudians—and the Claudians were from the top of the top drawer. This haughty clan liked to trace their ancestors right back to the founding of Rome. And so with this kind of blood and the influence of Augustus, the future of Tiberius was assured. This is so even though Augustus was not particularly fond of him.

Tiberius attended the finest schools and acquired an excellent education. And yet he was not happy because he was constantly being ordered about by his mother—and Augustus. In his youth he met the lovely Vipsania, daughter of another admiral, Marcus Agrippa. Both Tiberius and Vipsania enjoyed the sea. Soon they were married and were extremely happy. Then Augustus got another family-shattering idea.

Augustus had had three wives: Claudia, Scribonia, and Livia. But like Solomon, he had only one child, a daughter by Scribonia. This daughter, Julia, was the apple of his eye. When she was only fourteen, Augustus persuaded his sister Octavia to insist that her son Marcellus divorce his wife and marry Julia. Two years later Marcellus died and the attractive widow became the scandal of Rome. Augustus then forced forty-two-year-old Agrippa to divorce his wife and marry her.

Following Agrippa's death, Augustus decreed that Tiberius break with Vipsania and marry Julia. Tiberius did not want to do this for he was deeply attached to Vipsania—moreover Vipsania was pregnant. But Augustus had spoken and so Tiberius did what he was told. And this was to his sorrow, for Julia continued to have affairs with other men.

Soon, however, Augustus himself got disgusted with Julia. At a gay party, he astonished the guests by announcing that she had been banished to "a barren rock off the Campanian coast." But the damage to Tiberius—damage that he would avenge by killing his thousands—had already been done.

While Augustus was dying in A.D. 14, he realized that Tiberius was going to succeed him. He had already paved the way for this event by legally adopting him as his son. Still, Augustus was unhappy. As the attendants waited at the royal bed, he gasped: "Poor Rome, doomed to be masticated by those slow-moving jaws!"

Yes, Tiberius was slow of speech; but his mind was like a trap. He had carefully planned his future and he knew exactly what he was going to do. At first he pretended that he really didn't want the power of an emperor. He declared that he would much rather work with a number of rulers. But the Senate was not deceived. Said one courageous senator: "Some people are slow to do what they promise; you are slow to promise what you have already done."

Finally, and with fake reluctance, Tiberius agreed to become the new emperor. Even then, he made a subtle suggestion that he might resign at a later date! And since he was already 55, many believed that the date of his resignation was just a short time away. Soon the Senate began to vote him honors. But on each occasion he vetoed the bill; and this brought more honors.

Tiberius never remarried and his mother took advantage of this by moving in with him. In the palace, she practically told him what to do; and she felt she had a right to do this, for she had paved the way to his success. Dio, a Roman biographer, says: "But not satisfied to rule on equal terms with him, she wished to assert a superiority over him . . . and undertook to manage everything like a sole ruler." As a dutiful son, he listened—and obeyed. But as he grew into his sixties his mother became intolerable. In desperation, he moved her into a separate house. Like other Romans, Tiberius was superstitious and believed in omens. This tendency was a natural one for his mother was always listening to astrologers and using other means to discover the future. "Just before his (Tiberius') birth," wrote Suetonius, "Livia had tried various means of foretelling whether her child would be male or female; one was to take an egg from underneath a broody hen and warm it alternately in her own hands and in those of her women—and she successfully hatched a cock-chick which already had a fine comb."

Tiberius believed in astrology; and like many who have a weakness of which they are ashamed, he soothed his conscience by persecuting others. All astrologers were banned from Rome unless they agreed to make no more predictions. Those who disobeyed were sold into slavery. Likewise, he banished all foreign religions—especially those of Egypt and all forms of Judaism. And when a Jewish youth was of military age he was sent to a camp in an unhealthy region, the hope being that he would acquire a fatal disease.

All of his laws were not damaging. He fought crime by increasing the police force; and he kept gladiator duels to a minimum. Tiberius was extremely economical with the public treasury. Foreign dignitaries were often shocked by his economies. Often at banquets—even the best—he served leftovers! If one side of a boar had been served one day, he saw no reason why the other side should not be served the next. At the time he took office there were one hundred million sesterces in the Treasury. By the end of his rule there were almost three billion sesterces in the accounts.

On the surface, Tiberius appeared a humble man. When bills were presented in the Senate which would change the names of the months of September and October to Tiberius and Livius in honor of himself and his mother, he refused to have anything to do with them. "What would you do should there be thirteen Caesars?" he demanded. But beneath that smooth surface he was cunning, cruel, grasping.

As the affairs of Rome started to improve, the private life of Tiberius began to disintegrate. In his 67th year he moved to the Island of Capri and began a life of utter debauchery that is probably unexcelled in history. Luke tells us that John the Baptist was preaching in the wilderness during "the fifteenth year of Tiberius Caesar" (Luke 3:1). He also tells us that Jesus was baptized during this period when He "began to be about thirty years of age" (3:23). And so as Jesus was gathering His disciples, healing the sick, and then dying on the cross, the leader of the Roman Empire—an old man in his seventies— was giving himself to unnatural vice.

Under his leadership, Capri became such a wicked place it was sneered at as "Caprineum." The palace was filled with lewd pictures and statues; and the vilest type of pornography was brought to him. His wickedness was so gross and so continuous—(it especially involved children)—that it is far too revolting to write about. All that can be said is that his mind was as corrupt as a sewer.

Tiberius felt especially inspired to protect the name of Augustus. When a man was accused of removing the head from a statue of his stepfather, he ordered the man executed. This lust to kill increased with his age. Suetonius makes the almost unbelievable remark that "People could now be executed for beating a slave or changing their clothes close to an image of Augustus, or for carrying a ring or coin bearing Augustus' head into a privy. . . . The climax came when a man died merely for letting an honor be voted him by the native town council on the same day that honors had once been voted to Augustus."

Tiberius was so corrupt that talented men wrote poems about him. One which must have been scrawled in many a back alley had this verse:

> He is not thirsty for neat wine
> As he was thirsty then,
> But warms him up a tastier cup—
> The blood of murdered men.

At the time of the resurrection of Jesus Christ, someone asked Tiberius what he thought about it; and he was alleged to have replied that he didn't believe it, for the Senate had not voted on whether or not Jesus was divine!

A few days before his death, the Capri lighthouse collapsed during an earthquake. Superstitious Tiberius felt certain that this was an omen indicating that he was near the end. From then on, he was troubled by dreadful dreams.

Death finally came in his seventy-ninth year. The details of his passing are wrapped in mystery. But since those details are closely connected with the career of his successor, Caligula, we will leave them for the next chapter.

Chapter 3

Caligula, the Tyrant

One of Caligula's best friends was Herod Agrippa, the impulsive nephew of Herod Antipas, the Herod before whom Jesus stood on the day of His trial.

Herod Agrippa was twenty years older than the teenage Caligula, the youngest son of Germanicus and grandnephew of Tiberius. But instead of being a barrier, this span of years merely enabled the older one to pass on the knowledge of more vice. Moreover, Caligula was a zealous student!

While the two were enjoying a chariot ride, the conversation drifted onto the subject of what Caligula would do after he had inherited the throne. Knowing that Tiberius would be merciless to anyone who longed for his death, the two friends spoke in whispers. Unfortunately for himself, Herod was carried away with enthusiasm.

Speaking a little too loudly, Herod suggested that after the death of Tiberius, it would be easy to take care of Gemellus. (Gemellus, the only grandson of Tiberius was the product of the marriage between Drusus, son of Tiberius, and his cousin Livia, sister of Germanicus.)The driver overheard the remark and repeated it to the Emperor. Tiberius immediately ordered

Herod's arrest. Some time later, in the spring of A.D. 37, an old friend visited Herod in prison. Speaking in Hebrew, he whispered in his ear, "The old lion is dead."

Overjoyed, Herod ordered a feast to which he invited all the prison officials. But just as they started to gorge, word came that Tiberius wasn't dead after all. The "guests" responded by shoving away all the dishes and binding their flabbergasted host in chains!

The report, however, was merely an exaggeration. Although still alive, Tiberius was on his deathbed. And as he rolled and tossed, he prayed to his gods for direction in choosing a new emperor. Finally he decided that he would summon both Caligula and Gemellus to his bedside in the morning, and that the one who arrived first would receive the throne.

Curiously, Gemellus overslept and dallied at his breakfast. Thus, Caligula arrived first at the royal bedside. Tiberius was furious, for he distrusted Caligula.

Caligula was tall, slender, had thin hair on his head, and his tight little mouth was inclined to open to one side. He had heavy brows, unblinking eyes; and sometimes when he spoke the words slipped out in a snarl.

But since Caligula was the first one to his side, Tiberius had no alternative but to make him the new emperor. A few minutes later the old man closed his eyes, and it was thought that he was dead. Soon the room was packed with well-wishers. But just as they were congratulating Caligula, Tiberius sat up and demanded something to eat.

Caligula was terrified. He feared his great-uncle might have witnessed his unspeakable joy and changed his mind. The courtiers, too, were uneasy, for they knew that one twitch of those powerful lips could send them to their deaths. Slowly, one by one, they slipped into the corridor and hid in other rooms.

But Caligula was not one to risk his future on the whims of a dying man. He grabbed at the Emperor's signet ring. If he could only slip this on his finger, it would symbolize the transfer of power! But Tiberius clenched his fist and would not let him have it. Exactly what followed, no one knows. But it is surmised by a number of authorities that Caligula smothered him—perhaps by ordering the blankets over his head, or with a pillow.

The moment Tiberius was clearly dead, Caligula gave his first official order. And that was that the servant who had witnessed the old man's death be executed at once.

And thus Caligula became the ruler of the Roman Empire!

Caligula, however, was not his real name. His real name was Gaius Caesar Augustus Germanicus. The nickname Caligula— Little Boot—was given him by the soldiers because when he was young he dressed as an enlisted man and wore *caligae*— soldier's boots. His grandmother on his father's side was a daughter of Antony; and his grandmother on his mother's side was the daughter of Augustus. With these two conflicting streams in his veins, and with the descendants of these two rival families about him, Caligula was as taut as the string of a bow.

During the first seven months of his reign, Caligula was a model of moderation. He assured the Senate that he would listen to them—that he was their servant. He gave great public banquets and was generous with his opposition. But during late autumn he became dangerously ill. On his recovery, he was a different man.

Soon he fell in love with his own sister Drusilla. Since she was already married, he forced her to leave her husband and marry him. He then told the shocked Roman society that this was perfectly all right, and that no one should complain. He argued that the Pharaohs had done this and since Rome ruled Egypt it was perfectly legal for him.

This argument did not convince his grandmother, Antonia; and since she refused to keep silent, he ordered her to poison herself. He then had her cremated in front of his dining room window. As the smoke curled up before him, he shrugged.

About this time Gemellus came to dinner smelling of cough medicine. Caligula instantly accused him of having taken an antidote to protect himself from poison; and since this reflected on him, he ordered Gemellus to commit suicide. The eighteen-year-old youth complied by falling on his sword.

Ordering people to kill themselves now became a hobby with Caligula. Again and again he ordered all sorts of people in many strata of society to take their own lives. And each time, as they obeyed, Caligula's sense of divinity increased. When sitting at dinner with a number of friends, he suddenly burst out laughing. On being asked the reason for his mirth, he replied: "I was just thinking that by a single nod of my head I could have all of your throats cut!" The remark had a sobering effect.

While he embraced either his wife or the lady of his momentary fancy, he liked to remark: "Off comes this beautiful head whenever I give the word."

Caligula's contempt for the masses was complete. And in order to dramatize this contempt, he officially announced that his favorite horse, Incitatus, was a consul. Moreover, he assigned an impressive house and a retinue of servants to the horse. Parties were thrown for distinguished guests with the horse acting as host. These extremes, however, did not satisfy his twisted sense of humor; and so he assigned the horse to a temple and made him a priest!

Always fond of the exotic, he reversed the orders of Tiberius and made the worship of the Egyptian goddess Isis one of the legal cults of Rome. Having no doubts about his rights to satisfy every whim, he filled his life with debauchery. While attending the wedding of a friend, he decided that he should have the bride himself; and so he insisted on marrying her while the groom stood by in speechless astonishment. Then tiring of her, he obtained a divorce.

Caligula loved auctions so much he frequently mounted the table and assumed the role of auctioneer. He especially loved to sell slaves and gladiators; and sometimes he forced the rich to attend his sales. On one occasion, a certain aristocrat who had been forced to attend, nodded in sleep. Caligula interpreted each nod as a bid. When the unfortunate man awakened, he found he had purchased thirteen gladiators for the enormous sum of 9,000,000 sesterces.

Being a colorful man, Caligula inspired colorful stories. And today we must keep in mind that many of these stories originated with writers who loved tall tales. Nonetheless, even though Dio Cassius wrote two hundred years after Caligula's death, Tacitus loathed all emperors, and Suetonius had an ear tuned to the bizarre, their records are hard to disprove. This is because they fit into the times. For example, it was declared that ordinary water was not good enough for Caligula's bath, and so he bathed in perfume and spent 10,000,000 sesterces on a single banquet. This kind of extravagance soon exhausted the ample treasury left by Tiberius. In order to raise more revenue, Caligula taxed almost everything. When this did not bring in sufficient funds, he had rich men condemned for treason and then confiscated their estates. The executioners who led these victims to their deaths were instructed to kill them "by numerous slight wounds, so that they will feel that they are dying."

According to Suetonius, when a meat shortage developed in the zoo, Caligula decreed that all "bald-headed prisoners" be fed to the animals. This was to keep the various beasts in good health. But we must remember that Suetonius was a gossip, and maybe this is mere gossip!

At the beginning of his spectacular career, Caligula announced that he was a god, fully equal to Jupiter. He then ordered the heads on the statues of the gods to be removed and to be replaced with replicas of his own head. Next, he had a thunder machine constructed, and answered "Jove's thunder" with his own, peal for peal. But sometimes the natural thunder was too much for him. On such occasions he crawled whimpering under the bed!

Many of the countries ruled by Caligula found no difficulty

in worshiping him, for they already had many gods and it was easy to add another. The Jews, however, refused to worship anyone other than Jehovah. This uncompromising stand brought a lot of persecution down on their heads. Because of this, Philo of Alexandria headed a deputation to see the Emperor.

Philo and his colleagues tried to explain their position to Caligula. But he refused to listen to them seriously. Nevertheless, because of Caligula's friendship with Herod Agrippa, he did not persecute them. However, in order to tease them, he ordered his statue placed in the Holy of Holies in Jerusalem!

This order was never obeyed because of a tidal wave of disapproval from the Jews; but it did provide Caligula with many a light moment.

By the time he was 29, Caligula was an old man. His excesses had drained his vitality; and he was hated by almost the entire Roman Empire. On January 24, A.D. 41, he made the mistake of insulting an officer in his bodyguard once too often. This officer, Cassius Chaerea, yanked out his sword and slashed the Emperor on his shoulder. Then, stunned by what he had done, Chaerea stood to one side and stared.

It seemed impossible that he could have done such a thing.

But as he stared, other members of the guard swooped down on the tyrant and finished him off with their swords.

And thus ended the career of Caligula. Looking back, most historians agree that he was insane.

Chapter 4

Herod the Great

He murdered his wife, executed his sons, attempted to kill Jesus, and twice tried to commit suicide. Nevertheless, history calls him Herod the Great. And in a sense, history is right!

Grossly immoral, he had ten wives—two of them nieces—and had affairs with his own eunuchs. Likewise, he was the source of the numerous Herods who cast such sinister shadows throughout the New Testament. Sorting and identifying these Herods is an intriguing task. But it is worthwhile—even though it is something like learning the names of different types of spiders.

Undoubtedly the best way to understand the Herods is to start with Herod the Great. But first we must think of his grandfather Antipas and his father Antipater.

Antipas was the first of the Herods to come to public notice. We do not know much about him. He was, however, designated "general over all Idumea." The beginnings of his son Antipater are also shrouded in mystery. But we do know that he held high political position and that he lived in Jerusalem around 67 B.C. Amazingly, Antipater was not a racial Jew, nor was his wife Cypros! Antipater, father of Herod the Great, the King of the Jews, was an Edomite. These descendants of Esau occupied the deserts of Southern Judea. And from the beginning of their existence they had been antagonistic to Israel. They had a habit of swooping down on Jewish settlements and making slaves of the people.

Indeed, the Edomites were such a problem they were denounced by the prophets: Amos, Joel, Obadiah, and Ezekiel. A psalmist also pointedly wrote: "Remember, O Lord, the children of Edom in the day of Jerusalem; who said, Rase it, rase it, even to the foundation thereof" (Psalms 137:7).

The Edomites, however, had been conquered in the second century B.C. by the Jewish high priest and king, John Hyrcanus. Hyrcanus then forced them to be circumcised and to become Jews. Thus, Antipater was a Jew merely because his ancestors had been forced into Judaism.

And yet even more damaging to the children of Antipater in the sight of the Jews was the fact that his wife was a Nabatean Arab! And even worse, according to Jewish law, the children took the nationality of the mother. Still, this is not the end of the handicaps that were heaped on the shoulders of the future King of the Jews. Antipater had five children. Four of these: Phasael, Joseph, Salome, and Pheroras had solid Jewish names. But alas, when the King-to-be of the Jews made his appearance in 73 B.C. he was shackled with the Greek name Herod!

With a Greek name, an Arab mother, and an Edomite father, young Herod should have stayed out of politics—especially Jewish politics. But Herod possessed an agile mind and such hindrances meant nothing to him.

After clearing the Mediterranean of pirates in 67 B.C., Pompey—brilliant and yet arrogant Roman general and statesman—headed for Jerusalem. The pirates he had faced were so brazen they had gilded masts, purple sails, and used silver-plated oars. But he had conquered their one thousand ships in a mere three months, and now he was confident that he could deal with the Holy City.

Fearing for the life of his ten-year-old son Herod, Antipater sent the lad along with his mother to Petra. There, the boy was undoubtedly taunted by the Arabian children as being an Arab. These taunts were like a knife and they twisted deep into his heart. And then he had an experience that influenced his entire future life.

Petra being a few miles south of the Dead Sea and Qumran, home of the Essenes (and where, two thousand years later, the Dead Sea Scrolls were found at the northwest end of this body of water)—quite likely the Essenes were a familiar sight on the streets. The story is told that while on his way to school, Herod was surprised when a distinguished Essene by the name of Menahem approached. While patting him on his behind, the old man said that he was glad to meet the future King of the Jews.

"But I am just a commoner," replied Herod. He was a little startled for Menahem had a reputation of knowing the future.

"You will nevertheless become the king," assured the old man, "and you will reign happily because God has found you worthy." Then, arching his great brows, he added a word of caution. "Your most reasonable course of action, which will bring you a good reputation, will be to practice justice and piety toward God. *But I know you will not be such a person.*"

Young Herod grew rapidly into a tall, good-looking young man. He had powerful shoulders, was good with a bow and arrow; and he was an expert with the javelin. In his leisure time he went hunting.

In the following years when Julius Caesar became master of Rome and her colonies, he made Antipater ruler of Palestine in 47 B.C. In turn, Antipater made his eldest son, Phasael, governor of Jerusalem and Herod the ruler of Galilee. Thus, Herod was in politics. And he had started near the top.

About this time, Herod met Mark Antony at Petra. Antony was a military genius, but he was utterly corrupt, and was quite

31

willing to use anyone who could further his career. Soon, he and Herod became lifelong friends. Alas, this friendship nearly destroyed Herod.

Always conscious that he was only a commoner and not even a racial Jew, Herod wished he could hide his origins from the public. This, of course, was impossible. But there was a way to help his personal cause. If he could marry into the highest circles, the glow of his wife would shield him. And so he began to look around. Soon his eyes fell on the exquisitely beautiful Mariamne.

Mariamne was the granddaughter of John Hyrcanus II, a Maccabean—and the present high priest! The Maccabees had won the nation a former independence from the Seleucids, and thus being related to them would be a dazzling honor. Forthwith, he divorced his wife Doris, an Edomite like himself, and went after Mariamne. With his considerable charm, they were soon engaged. The heights were still in the distance, but he was in the foothills—and was climbing.

And then in 44 B.C. the peace of the world was shattered by the murder of Julius Caesar in the Roman Senate on the Ides (fifteenth) of March. Judea was shocked by Caesar's death. Suetonius wrote: "Public grief was enhanced by crowds of foreigners lamenting in their fashion, especially Jews who loved Caesar for the friendship he had shown them." Julius Caesar had exempted Jews from military service; had allowed them to send money to the Temple; and had restored to them the vital port of Joppa.

Although shocked at learning he was not to be the successor to Caesar, Mark Antony joined forces with Octavian to defeat the assassins—Brutus and Cassius. And in the famous battle of Philippi—where Paul founded the first European church a century later—Antony won the victory and saved Octavian's life. Now with Brutus and Cassius dead, the Triumvirate made up of Octavian, Lepidus, and Antony, took over their previously agreed assignments. With the eastern section a part of his rule, Antony sailed up the Orontes River to Antioch.

At his headquarters in the Daphne Park of Antioch, Antony faced a huge delegation of Jews. After listening patiently to their complaints about Herod, he turned to Hyrcanus.

"Who are the best rulers?" he demanded.

"Herod and his party," replied the high priest.

Then in Judge Roy Bean style, Antony immediately appointed Herod and his brother Phasael as tetrarchs. The word means *ruler of a fourth*. This meant that they were now official rulers of a part of the territory. Antony also recognized Hyrcanus, the Maccabean, as *ethnark—ruler of the nation*.

Herod left with a light heart. His fortunes were rising; and within a short time Mariamne would be his. Indeed, she might even become a queen. Other troubles, however, were brewing.

By 40 B.C.—only two years after the battle of Philippi—the Parthians, an Indo-European race from what is now Iran—conquered Syria. But these lustful warriors with their frizzed beards were not satisfied with just Syria. Soon they began to covet Jerusalem. Jerusalem, however, had thick walls and fierce defenders. The realistic Parthians knew this, and so they decided on intrigue. And for this purpose, they had an ideal pawn—Antigonus, great grandson of Hyrcanus I.

Antigonus was a frustrated Hasmonean. (The rule by the Maccabean family was known as the Hasmonean Dynasty.) Along with his father, Aristobulus II, the last of the independent Hasmonean kings, and other members of the royal family, Antigonus had been sent as a prisoner to Rome by Pompey after his conquest of Jerusalem in 63 B.C.

Six years later, Antigonus and his father escaped. But soon they were captured and sent back to Rome. After a while, however, he and the other members of the family were allowed to return to Judea. Next, he went to Rome and pled with Julius Caesar to be made king of Judea. Julius Caesar turned down his request for he preferred Antipater, the father of Herod.

The Parthians approached Antigonus with an attractive

offer. If he would cooperate with them, they would put him on the Judean throne in the place of his uncle, John Hyrcanus II. Antigonus was delighted with this offer, and responded with a bargaining point of his own: If they succeeded in putting him on the throne, he would give them one thousand talents (over a million dollars) and five hundred highborn women. And among those highborn women, according to Josephus, would be the wives and daughters of Herod and his brothers! Following this sinister agreement, the Parthians began their advance.

Soon Acco (later known as Acre) fell, and then, filled with confidence, they headed toward Jerusalem. Here, skirmishes and then pitched battles were fought in the streets. At the feast of Pentecost thousands of armed pilgrims pulled out their daggers and helped Antigonus. Hard pressed, Herod lost all the city with the exception of the palace area. At this point the Parthian general persuaded Phasael—Herod's older brother—and Hyrcanus II to leave and negotiate with Barzaphranes, the Parthian king, then in Galilee.

Herod feared trickery and advised against going. But Phasael and Hyrcanus II would not listen. In Galilee, just as Herod had feared, the men were arrested and loaded with chains. Antigonus then went one step further. His uncle Hyrcanus had been high priest for thirty-six years, and Antigonus felt certain that this was much too long. And so he persuaded the Parthians to snip off his ears and exile him in Babylon. This mutilation served to keep Hyrcanus from being high priest again, for according to Leviticus 21:17, a priest had to be without blemish. Knowing he couldn't win, Herod, in Jerusalem, assembled his mother, Mariamne and her mother, the five hundred ladies whom Antigonus was going to give away, along with thousands of others. When it was pitch black, he led them through the Dung Gate and out of the city. About nine thousand—some authorities say ten thousand—escaped with him. This escape is hard to explain, for he was guarded by ten Parthian officers and two hundred cavalrymen. Nevertheless, he escaped!

Recently a tetrarch and now a fugitive, Herod's arrogance sagged to a new low. When the wagon bearing his mother overturned, he was so shaken he started to commit suicide. But when he learned that she was safe, he changed his mind.

By dawn, the Parthians and Jews discovered his escape and started after him. They caught up with him at a place known now as Herodion just southeast of Bethlehem, about seven miles from Jerusalem. Knowing they faced slavery if they lost, the men out-performed themselves and routed the enemy. Farther south, five miles beyond Hebron, Herod's men joined those of his younger brother, Joseph. It was here they decided to disband the troops and lodge their families at Masada. Joseph agreed to guard them with eight hundred men.

Some years before, the Hasmonian ruler Jonathan had erected a fortress on this rocky cliff. With keen foresight, Herod saw the advantages of this stronghold and made it a place of refuge complete with storehouses and supplies. Josephus tells the story. "Upon the top of the hill, Jonathan the high priest first of all built a fortress, and called it Masada; after which the rebuilding of this place employed the care of King Herod to a great degree; he also built a wall around the entire top of the hill, seven furlongs long; it was composed of white stones; and its height was twelve and its breadth twelve cubits; there were also erected upon that wall thirty-eight towers, each of them fifty cubits high. . . .

"Moreover, he built a palace therein at the western ascent. . . . Now the wall of the palace was very high and very strong, and had at its four corners towers sixty cubits high. . . . He had also cut many and great pits, as reservoirs of water, out of the rocks. . . . "

Now safe in this fortress, Herod tried to get allies. Failing in this, he managed to sail for Rome. There, both Octavian and Antony listened with sympathy. Deeply moved, they presented Herod to the Senate; and the Senate voted him the title King of the Jews. But being voted king, and actually being king were two different matters, for Antigonus was firmly in control.

Herod, however, had his appointment from Rome, and so therefore he summoned the Romans to help—and eventually they came. In the winter of 37 B.C. Herod laid siege to Jerusalem. The trees in the area were cut down and formed into siege engines; and like Pompey, he attacked from the north—a side unprotected by ravines.

In the midst of the siege, Herod solemnized his vows with Mariamne. He needed all the help he could get!

At the end of five months the city fell on a day of fasting. Antigonus was placed in chains and dispatched to Antony in Antioch. There, he was scourged on a cross and later beheaded.

Herod was now thirty-six and was on the throne—but he was not quite supreme. No, the real power was in the hands of the high priest. But Herod had a way to manipulate that office. Cleverly he recalled Hyrcanus II from exile. Having been mutilated, Hyrcanus could not be high priest. Still, the old man could lend influence—especially to his granddaughter's husband. Next, he had Ananel, an obscure priest from Mesopotamia, assigned the position. The understanding, of course, was that Herod was to be consulted on all major decisions. It seemed an ideal arrangement.

Mariamne, however, had other ideas! She wanted a high priest in her family—and there was her brother Aristobulus III. True, the lad was only seventeen or eighteen. However, he was extremely good looking and according to Leviticus, age was not considered.

Herod did not want him. And so Mariamne went over his head and appealed to Antony. Now Herod was a realist. He knew Antony; and he feared the good looks of the boy might overwhelm the man. There was even a remote possibility that the boy might eventually be made king. But because of pressure, and because he had thought of a way out of the tangle, Herod yielded.

Aristobulus was extremely popular. Dressed in glittering

robes, he was a stunning sight. Moreover, he was a Maccabee. Herod watched; ground his teeth, swallowed; forced a smile— and waited.

Herod's time to act came immediately after the Feast of Tabernacles. On an extremely hot day, he led Aristobulus aside during a feast at Jericho. He then suggested a swim. Late in the evening, while the water was covered with shadows, someone held the high priest's head under until he drowned.

Ananel was then returned to office. Herod was now all-powerful. He covered the drowning by staging an elaborate funeral. But Mariamne knew; and she refused to forgive her husband.

The ship of state was now moving smoothly again. Herod decided this was the time to settle old scores. For years he had hated the Sanhedrin because while he was ruling Galilee they had tried him for executing a brigand without first consulting them. He decided the time had come for a purge. Remembering those who had been against him, he had them executed— all forty-five of them! In addition, their entire estates were confiscated. He then nominated another forty-five. This was so the body could have its required seventy-one members.

Herod was now a confident, swaggering dictator. And then unexpectedly his world almost disintegrated. Augustus Caesar—Octavian's new title—declared war on Antony and Cleopatra. Herod immediately threw his weight on the side of Antony. Alas, he guessed wrong! Antony and Cleopatra were so utterly defeated in the sea battle of Actium off the west coast of Greece, they committed suicide.

Terrified by his awkward position, Herod called on Augustus Caesar on the Island of Rhodes. Thoroughly humiliated, the King of the Jews removed his crown and begged for mercy. His only resource was his considerable charm. Smiling bravely, he explained that he had made efforts to get Antony to leave Cleopatra. Augustus listened, and being a practical man, forgave. Herod was bloody. Still, he could handle the troublesome Jews.

"Put on your crown!" he ordered.

Herod replaced his crown, but he remained an unhappy man. Mariamne was unforgiving. The rift increased. Herod accused her of adultery. Finally, he ordered a trial. Then he had her executed. Now, his personal troubles really began; for Herod really loved Mariamne. Again and again he rushed around his palace calling, "Mariamne! Mariamne!" He fled to the desert for peace, but peace eluded him. On his return he became morbid, sullen. Then a new fear dominated him.

What would he do if a sympathetic public wanted Mariamne's sons to be rulers in his place. And this was a real possibility, for they had royal blood! It was a problem that had to be settled at once. Herod did not hesitate. He ordered them executed.

They were strangled.

Upon hearing of these murders, it is said that Augustus Caesar commented, "It is better to be Herod's pig than his son." This remark had grim humor in it, for as a practicing Jew, Herod would not kill a pig!

Sooner than he hoped, Herod began to age. He dyed his hair; took special baths; married new women, including Mariamne II; and went on expensive trips. Nothing satisfied. Thinking the end was close, he made a will which named his elder son—by his first wife, Doris—Antipater his successor. This relieved his mind for the moment. Then in his sixty-eighth or sixty-ninth year, the wise men from the east came to Jerusalem. These sages talked about a star and a babe who was to be King of the Jews.

The words of these men from the east so alarmed him, he sent for them. One wonders about his thoughts as he peered into their faces. Did he remember the other wise man, Menahem? Also, the mention of Bethlehem must have revived old memories; for when he escaped from Jerusalem with the nine thousand, it was near this city where he was overtaken.

Such questions cannot be answered. But the New Testament relates that Herod ordered all the children in Bethlehem from two years and under to be slaughtered in an attempt to kill the future King of the Jews. Secular history is silent about this episode. Still, it so fits Herod's character we are forced to believe it.

As he neared seventy, Herod lost patience with his son, Antipater, had him arrested, and changed his will. Next, he fled to Jericho seeking relief in this tropical resort city from the disease that had gripped him. While peeling an apple, he suddenly raised the blade to stab himself. A stronger hand, however, stopped him.

News of the suicide attempt reached Antipater in the dungeon. Assuming that his father was dead, he tried to get the jailer to release him. Instead, the jailer reported to Herod. In a fit of rage, Herod raised himself on his elbow and ordered his son's immediate execution. He then drew up a new will making his remaining sons rulers. Antipas was to be tetrarch of Galilee and Perea; Archelaus king of Judea, Samaria and Idumea; Philip tetrarch of Gaulonitis, Trachonitis and Paneas. And to his sister Salome he left some cash, some groves and two cities.

Four days later, suffering from lack of breath, a gangrenous and maggoty scrotum, dreadful itching, malfunction of the kidneys, ulceration of the bowels, and many other things, he died. He died on March 13, 4 B.C. The date is accurate because on that night there was an eclipse of the moon as mentioned by Josephus. (This proves that Jesus was born before the year 1 B.C., for Herod was alive during Jesus' first years.) Archelaus provided an elaborate funeral. The masses attended. But it was hard for them to weep!

The career of Herod the Great was summed up well by Joseph Klausner. Said he: "He stole to the throne like a fox, ruled like a tiger, and died like a dog."

Augustus Caesar approved the will. And thus, those who were given power to rule, received it. Unfortunately, many of the acts of the heirs were evil and cruel. Today, these descendants of Herod are remembered mostly because of the early Christians they tried to eliminate.

Chapter 5

The Descendants of Herod

Altogether, including Herod the Great, seven Herods appear in the New Testament. But since their dramatic intrigues and erratic behavior are so complicated, we do not have space to write about them in depth. Instead, we will sketch their lives in proportion to their importance.

Herod Antipas

Herod Antipas—referred to as Herod in the New Testament—was the son of Herod the Great and Malthace, a Samaritan wife. This means that he had even less Jewish blood than his father! In spite of this, Antipas is mentioned more often in the New Testament than any other Herod. And so sordid was his character, the Pharisees warned Jesus that Antipas sought to kill Him, Jesus responded dubbing him "that fox" (Luke 13:31,32).

According to his father's last will, Antipas was made tetrarch of Galilee. He was never popular and his prestige sank to a new low when he married his niece Herodias, the former wife of his half brother, Philip—son of one of Herod's ten wives, Cleopatra. (Herodias was the daughter of another half-brother, Aristobulus.)

This double-sin had inspired John the Baptist to reprimand him face to face (Matthew 14:1-4). Later, when Salome, daughter of Herodias by Philip, danced before Antipas, he was so drunk with desire he impulsively agreed to give Herodias anything she wished. His wife's request was immediate. She demanded the head of John the Baptist on a tray. Moreover, although Herod regretted his rash promise, he complied at once.

Herod Antipas is also the Herod to whom Pilate sent Jesus during His trial. Luke has given us a graphic picture of their confrontation. "And when Herod saw Jesus, he was exceeding glad: for he was desirous to see him of a long season, because he had heard many things of him; and he hoped to have seen some miracle done by him" (Luke 23:8).

Following his one-way conversation with Jesus—it was one-way because Jesus refused to answer—"Herod with his men of war set him at nought, and mocked him, and arrayed him in a gorgeous robe, and sent him again to Pilate" (verse 11).

Like his father, Antipas was an enthusiastic builder. He continued many of the projects his father had started; and he built a new seaport on the southwest shore of Galilee and named it Tiberias in honor of the Roman emperor. He also rebuilt Sepphoris some four miles north of Nazareth—a place where Jesus and Joseph may have worked as carpenters.

Herodias soon became jealous of her half-brother Agrippa I—son of Aristobulus and grandson of Herod the Great and Mariamne I. This was because he had been made king of Judea. In order to advance her husband Antipas, she persuaded him to go with her to Rome and ask Emperor Caligula for a crown. But before they arrived, Agrippa had sent word to Caligula that Antipas was in secret league with the Parthians. Because Agrippa and Caligula were old friends, the youthful emperor chose to believe Agrippa.

Antipas was exiled in A.D. 39. And it is interesting to note that this was only a handful of years after he had mocked Jesus. No one is quite certain as to the place of exile. In one passage Josephus says that it was in Gaul, and in another passage he states that it was in Spain. Herodias shared his exile.

Agrippa I

It is said that Agrippa I—commonly called King Agrippa—was seen standing and weeping in the synagogue. Why? Because he had just read Deuteronomy 17:15. That pivotal passage says: "Thou shalt in any wise set him king over thee, whom the Lord God shall choose: one from among thy brethren shalt thou set king over thee: *thou mayest not set a stranger over thee, which is not thy brother*" (italics added).

Agrippa was deeply concerned over the fact that his grandfather, Herod the Great, was not a real Jew. Experts in the Scripture, however, comforted him by pointing out that his grandmother Mariamne was as blue-blooded a Jew as one could find, for she was the granddaughter of the great John Hyrcanus! They also pointed out that a Jewish child always takes the nationality of the mother.

Perhaps it was this conflict in his heart that made Agrippa so cruel. He is the one who put James the son of Zebedee to death. When he saw that this pleased the Jews, he arrested Peter and would have done the same to him except for his escape (Acts 12:1-16).

Having gone to school in Rome, and having been a close friend of Caligula, he was inclined to be conceited. His death came as suddenly as the death he had meted out to James. Here is Luke's description: "And upon a set day Herod, arrayed in royal apparel, sat upon his throne, and made an oration unto them. And the people gave a shout, saying, It is the voice of a god, and not of a man. And immediately the angel of the Lord smote him, because he gave not God the glory: and he was eaten of worms, and gave up the ghost" (Acts 12:21-23).

Josephus confirms this painful death and adds that he died in his fifty-fourth year.

Agrippa II

This Herod was the son of Agrippa I, and a full brother to Bernice and Drusilla. Herod the Great was his great grandfather. New Testament readers are well aquainted with this Agrippa, for he is the one before whom Paul presented his case at Caesarea.

Luke reports the beginning of this encounter in Acts 25:23. "And on the morrow, when Agrippa was come, and Bernice, with great pomp, and was entered into the place of hearing, with the chief captains, and principal men of the city, at Festus' commandment Paul was brought forth."

Paul had respect for Agrippa's knowledge of the Jews. Said he: "I know thee to be expert in all customs and questions which are among the Jews: wherefore I beseech thee to hear me patiently" (26:30).

The courtroom that day must have been extremely tense, and many of the eyes were certainly focused on Bernice. Although the name Bernice means "bearer of victory," this sister of King Agrippa, or Herod Agrippa as he was also called, was a very wicked woman. She was married twice, was suspected of living incestuously with her brother Agrippa, and later, she became a mistress to Titus in Rome and openly lived with him in the palace.

In his defense, Paul outlined the story of his conversion. In this outline, he exclaimed: "Whereupon, O king Agrippa, I was not disobedient unto the heavenly vision" (Acts 26:19).

One can imagine the intensity with which the court listened to this dynamic man of Tarsus. As he summed up his plea, Paul became very bold and said: "King Agrippa, believest thou the prophets? I know that thou believest" (verse 27). To this trust, Agrippa replied—perhaps sarcastically: "Almost thou persuadest me to be a Christian" (verse 28).

Agrippa was living in Rome at the time of his father's death in A.D. 44. At the time, he was a mere youth of 17; and the Roman Emperor Claudius felt that he was too young to accept his father's throne. Accordingly, he remained in Rome. Then in A.D. 48 when his uncle, king of Chalcis died, Claudius gave him this throne on the western slope of Anti-Lebanon.

Agrippa II seems to have pleased Claudius and he thus transferred him to the former tetrarchy of Philip which contained Batanea, Trachonitis, and Gaulonitis. And later even more territory was put under his jurisdiction.

As war threatened between Judea and Rome, Agrippa tried to persuade the Jews not to fight. Unsuccessful in this, he fought on the Roman side with Vespasian. He was wounded at the siege of Gamala.

Following the destruction of Jerusalem in A.D. 70, Agrippa and Bernice moved to Rome. There, he was made a praetor. He died in A.D. 100.

Of the statements of Agrippa II which are recorded in Acts, he is especially remembered for his conclusion in regard to Paul. Said he: "This man might have been set at liberty, if he had not appealed to Caesar" (Acts 26:32).

Herod Archelaus

This Herod was the son of Herod the Great and Malthace— and thus a full brother of Herod Antipas. According to his father's will he was made Ethnarch of Judea, Samaria and Idumea.

This Herod appears in one of the nativity events. Having fled to Egypt with the infant Jesus, Joseph and Mary were returning home after the death of Herod the Great. "But when he [Joseph] heard that Archelaus did reign in Judaea in the room of his father Herod, he was afraid to go thither: notwithstanding, being warned of God in a dream, he turned aside into the parts of Galilee" (Matthew 2:22).

Archelaus was in serious trouble with the Jews from the beginning of his reign. Like other Herods, he was morally corrupt. He married Glaphyra, a former wife of his half brother Alexander. And what made this even worse in the eyes of the Jews was that Glaphyra had had three children by Alexander.

Josephus wrote: "But in the tenth year of Archelaus' government, both his brethren and the principal men of Judea and Samaria, not able to bear his barbarous and tyrannical usage of them, accused him before Caesar."

Augustus Caesar responded by exiling him in Gaul. His reign lasted only from 4 B.C. to A.D. 6. But like the other Herods, he dabbled in architecture. He is especially remembered for having rebuilt the royal palace in Jericho.

The exile of Archelaus was a turning point in Jewish history. From this time on the realm was ruled by procurators appointed by Rome.

Philip the Tetrarch

As we have seen, Herod the Great had two wives by the name of Mariamne. Likewise, he had two sons by the name of Philip!

The first Philip was the son of Mariamne II; and the second Philip was the son of Cleopatra. This Philip is called the tetrarch because his father's will made him ruler of Gaulonitis, Trachonitis, and Paneas. His only mention in the Gospels is Luke 3:1. "Now in the fifteenth year of the reign of Tiberius Caesar, Pontius Pilate being governor of Judea, and Herod being tetrarch of Galilee, and his brother Philip tetrarch of Ituraea and of the region of Trachonitis . . ."

This Philip was the founder of the Gentile city, Caesarea Philippi some fifty miles southwest of Damascus. It was at this place Simon Peter made his famous confession, "Thou art the Christ, the Son of the living God" (Matthew 16:16). When Philip died in A.D. 34, the lands he had ruled were assigned to Syria.

Historians rate him as the best of the Herods.

Philip of Rome

This Philip, son of Herod the Great and Mariamne II, is noted for three things. He was the first husband of Herodias who later married Herod Antipas; he was the father of Salome whose lascivious dance brought about the execution of John the Baptist; and he is also remembered because his father, in a fit of anger, removed his name from his will.

Without lands to rule, Philip lived in Rome and died in obscurity.

Chapter 6

Pontius Pilate—
He Used a Basin

Although most Christians lump Pontius Pilate together with Judas Iscariot, both Pilate and his wife are devoutly worshiped as saints in Ethiopia. Indeed, June 25 is their feast day. On that occasion, faithful members of the Ethiopic Christian Church are supposed to think *about* and pray *to* Saint Pilate and his wife!

The reason? Because at the trial of Jesus, Pilate washed his hands and said: "I am innocent of the blood of this just man."

A veil of legend and mystery has been flung around this Roman officer. But there are enough dependable references in secular history and in the New Testament to give us a reasonably definite profile. And so let us flip the centuries back to the Roman year, A.U.C. 784. (A.U.C. stands for *ab urbe condita,* meaning "since the founding of the city." The Roman calendar went back to the mythical founding of Rome by Romulus and Remus in 753 B.C.) On the 15th day of Nisan, according to the Jewish calendar, or Friday, April 7, in accordance with our modern calendar—we see Pilate dressed in his Roman toga occupying a regal chair placed on a stone landing near his judgment hall. (We might mention that this date is disputed by those who believe Jesus was crucified on Wednesday.) A man of fashion, his hair is closely cropped in the Roman way. Defiant guards, their feet astride and a spear in their right hands, stand stiffly on either side. It is about eight o'clock in the morning and Jerusalem is bathed in warm sunshine.

Pilate had reason to be happy. As the fifth procurator of Judea, Samaria, and Idumea, he was a privileged character. (Remember when Herod Archelaus was deposed in A.D. 6, the Romans began to appoint procurators to rule Judea.) Governors of distant provinces in the Roman Empire were not allowed to take their wives along. But an exception had been made with Pilate. Perhaps Claudia had insisted. As the granddaughter of the great Augustus Caesar and the illegitimate daughter of the third wife of Tiberius Caesar, she had influence in Rome!

But this morning Pilate's dark Roman eyes glistened with sullen anger. He was annoyed because of the Jews. Fearing defilement, they refused to come into the regular court as decent and proper men should do. He was also angry because the sight of a Jew—almost any Jew—reminded him of past experiences with them. And this mob brought to mind an experience of a near yesteryear.

Pilate—the name means javelin—was a man who couldn't stand to be different. In every Roman city, with the glaring exception of Jerusalem, images of Caesar were proudly displayed in prominent places. But the Jews would have none of this, for they were so against idolatry even images of Caesar were taboo. And since Tiberius was determined to keep trouble to a minimum, he allowed the Jews to have their way.

This irritated Pilate. He wanted Jerusalem to be like all other cities, and he was determined to have his way—even though he had to resort to trickery. During a dark night, he sent soldiers into Jerusalem and had images of Caesar raised at the fortress Tower of Antonia. The fortress was next to the Temple and thus he knew the Jews would be incensed. But since this was a fortified area, he reasoned that the Jews would not protest too vigorously for fear of summoning a reprisal from the Romans.

Ah, but Pilate did not know the Jews—not really. Upon the advice of Caiaphas they began to pour into Jerusalem and head for Caesarea, sixty miles away. And as they plodded toward the capital, they gathered followers. By the time they reached Pilate's home, there were seven thousand of them!

But Pilate was unimpressed with numbers. When asked to remove the images he flatly refused. The Jews, however, could be obstinate. They just camped at his door and prayed that God would change his mind.

Every time Pilate looked out the window he saw Jews. Every time a friend called, the friend saw Jews. And every time he went outside he both saw and heard Jews. It was unnerving. Nevertheless, he believed they would soon tire. But he was mistaken. They had a sacred cause and would not give in. Finally, on the sixth day, his will crumbled. He told their leaders that if they would go to the market place he would speak to them.

After the Jews had filed into the market, Pilate ordered it surrounded with soldiers—many of them vengeful Samaritans. Now with flashing armor to bolster his spirits, Pilate told the Jews cold-bloodedly that if they didn't quit pestering him about the images he would have them massacred.

Then Pilate had the surprise of his life. Here is how Josephus relates what happened: "But they threw themselves upon the ground, and laid their necks bare, and said they would take their death very willingly, rather than the wisdom of their laws should be transgressed."

Deeply moved, Pilate "commanded the images to be carried back from Jerusalem to Caesarea."

Thus, Caiaphas had his way!

The crowd that wouldn't enter the hall on the 15th day of

Nisan pushed Jesus to the front and demanded action. By this time the face of Jesus was swollen by the blows He had received. His hair was matted and there was dry spittal on His cheeks.

"What accusation do you bring against this man?" asked Pilate lifting his jeweled hand for silence.

The answer came with the suddenness of a cattle whip. "If he were not a malefactor, we would not have delivered him unto thee."

"Take Him and judge Him according to your own laws," said Pilate, squirming. He was determined to stay neutral and not get into another quarrel which might be reported to Rome.

"It is not lawful for us to put any man to death," replied a spokesman.

Getting to his feet, Pilate motioned for Jesus to enter with him into the ornate judgment hall. The two men were approximately the same age—both nearing the peak of their young manhood. After searching His face Pilate asked: "Art thou the King of the Jews?"

"To this end was I born, and for this cause came I into the world, that I should bear witness unto the truth. Every one that is of the truth heareth My voice."

"What is truth?" demanded Pilate, a little startled. He then stepped out onto the game-scarred pavement, took his seat, and said to the mob, "I find in him no fault at all."

Pilate's words were met with a hiss of violent protest. The determined priests struck their foreheads with their fists and the Roman soldiers instinctively reached for their weapons. Then Pilate got an idea—an idea that would shift the responsibility to another. Somewhere in one of the conversations he had heard the word Galilee.

"This case is not for me," he said smoothly, chuckling inwardly at his cleverness, "it should be taken to Herod, Tetrarch of Galilee!"

But Herod Antipas—son of Herod the Great—didn't want to make a decision either. There was no value in sticking out one's neck, especially if it could be severed by Tiberius Caesar. And so after clothing Jesus in a purple robe and making sport of Him, he returned Him to Pilate.

This time Pilate was more direct. He knew Jesus had never uttered a word against the Roman government, or even against paying taxes. Moreover, he knew within the privacy of his heart that Jesus was without guilt. And so he pointedly said, "Ye have brought this man unto me, as one that perverteth the people: and, behold, I, having examined him before you, have found no fault in this man touching those things whereof ye accuse him."

At this, the crowd went wild. Their eyes and voices lashed at him like a typhoon-ridden sea. Desperately Pilate scrounged his mind for a way out. Then he remembered that it was customary to set a prisoner free on the day of the Feast of the Passover. He cleared his throat in order to make a suggestion. But even before he could speak a servant handed him a note from his wife.

The terse note said: "Have nothing to do with this just man: for I have suffered many things this day in a dream because of Him."

Pilate's eyes dilated and he could feel his heart thumping beneath his toga. He clenched his fists until his knuckles were white. Then, with a grim effort to keep his voice from trembling, he informed the mob that he would like to release a prisoner in order to follow the Passover custom. Next, he described Barabbas, a notorious criminal. "Whether of the twain will ye that I release unto you?" he asked.

"Away with the man," replied the crowd in one loud, unified voice, "and release unto us Barabbas."

But Pilate was still not ready to make a decision. Perhaps he could satisfy the Jews by having Jesus scourged. And so he gave the order for what was known as halfway death.

At a whipping post, Syrian soldiers tired themselves as they swung at Him with metal-tipped whips. And since this was Roman scourging they did not have to stop with thirty-nine stripes.

Finally, when Jesus was so weak He could barely stand, He was returned to Pilate. Facing the crowd, the ex-cavalry officer lifted Jesus' hand and cried, "*Ecce homo* [Behold the man]!" The crowd, however, wanted to see Him on a cross. Nothing else would satisfy them. All at once, like a Greek chorus, they began to chant, "Crucify Him! Crucify Him! Crucify Him!"

"Why, what evil hath He done?"

"Crucify Him! Crucify Him! Crucify Him!" was the terrifying answer.

Pilate still hesitated. He looked into the distorted faces of the frenzied mob, and he thought of Tiberius Caesar and his strict orders to keep peace in Judea. The jaws of the irresistible force and immovable object were rapidly and surely drawing together. An open grave seemed to gape before him.

Luke tells us that Pilate questioned the mob a third time. But again, he received the same deafening, unreasoning answer, "Crucify Him! Crucify Him! Crucify Him!"

His will completely shattered, Pilate called for a basin of water. Next, he slowly washed his hands and slowly dried them. Forcing the words from his parched lips, he slowly muttered, "I am innocent of the blood of this just person: see ye to it" (Matthew 27:24).

As Jesus was being led away to be crucified, Pilate opened the police blotter to the place where the record of judgments was kept. There, with a high sun winking on his jeweled hand, he wrote, "Jesus of Nazareth, scourged and crucified. April— A.U.C. 784." Although we know that this was April 7, according to our modern calendar, it would have been a different date in the days of Pilate owing to changes in the calendar— especially those made by Pope Gregory.

Having been involved in such high drama, many legends concerning Pilate have emerged. Josephus, however, has given us some stories that must be true. One of these concerns a Samaritan who inspired a crowd of Samaritans to climb Mount Gerizim with the promise that he would show them some sacred vessels which Moses had hidden there. Common sense should have told them, however, that Moses had never been there because of his death on Mount Nebo—many miles away—before the people of Israel ever crossed Jordan into the Promised Land.

"So they came thither armed," wrote Josephus, "and thought the discourse of the man probable; and as they abode at a certain village, which was called Tirathaba, they got the rest together to them, and desired to go up the mountain in a great multitude together; but Pilate prevented their going up by seizing upon the roads with a great band of horsemen and footmen, who fell upon those that were gotten together in the village; and when it came to an action, some of them they slew, and others of them they put to flight, and took a great many alive, the principal of which, and also the most potent of those that fled away, Pilate ordered slain."

Following this affair, Vitellius—Pilate's immediate superior—ordered him to Rome. But before Pilate arrived, Tiberius passed away on March 16, A.D. 37.

What followed is a mystery. Some say that Pilate was beheaded by Caligula; others, that he was beheaded by Nero. And still others claim that he committed suicide. A strong tradition declares that his head is buried on Mount Pilatus above Lake Lucerne in Switzerland. It is also suggested that Pilate's ghost, unable to find sanctuary, often returns to the lake and that one can hear it trying to wash the blood from its hands!

Another persistent legend says that Claudia became a convinced Christian. This legend has been so strong she was canonized by the Greek Orthodox Church.

Chapter 7

Claudius, the Impossible

Perhaps because of the bloodthirstiness of Nero who followed him, and the eccentricities of Caligula who preceded him, Claudius is often neglected. This is a mistake, for Claudius—in his own impossible way—was as colorful as either of them. And since he ruled between A.D. 41 and 54—a time when Christian churches were being planted—his career is exceedingly important to students of the New Testament.

Born in Lyons in 10 B.C., Claudius was only a few years older than Jesus. But so strange was this mysterious man in his youth, his mother often described him as "a monster: a man whom Mother Nature had begun to work upon and then flung aside." And when she was upset with someone, she frequently exclaimed, "He's a bigger fool than even my son Claudius!"

The idea that Claudius was retarded was believed by the whole Imperial family. Deeply concerned, his great uncle, Augustus Caesar, wrote to the grandmother of Claudius about him. Said Augustus:

"My dear Livia,

"As you have suggested, I have now discussed with Tiberius

what we should do about your grandson Claudius at the coming Festival of Mars the Avenger. We both agreed that an immediate decision ought to be taken. The question is whether he has—shall I say?—full command of his five senses. . . .

"I am against his watching the games in the Circus from the Imperial box, where the eyes of the whole audience would be upon him . . . " (Suetonius in *The Twelve Caesars*).

Augustus Caesar practically ignored him; and when Uncle Tiberius came to the throne, he treated him in the same manner. Thus neglected by relatives, Claudius began to associate with an unsavory class. He became addicted to gambling, and was frequently seen drunk.

How, then, did Claudius become the emperor? The answer to that is one of the most unique stories in history. But first we must have a glimpse of his genealogy.

The father of Claudius was Nero Claudius Drusus—a famous general and the first Roman to navigate the North Sea. Drusus died a year after Claudius was born. His mother was the young Antonia, daughter of the sister of Augustus—Octavia. Claudius was, therefore, the great-nephew of Augustus.

The royal blood of Claudius may have been even richer than what appears because of a curious event. His paternal grandmother, Livia Drusilla—mother of Drusus—was divorced from her first husband Tiberius Claudius Nero in 38 B.C. She then married Octavian—the future Augustus. However, Drusus was born a mere three months after this second marriage. And so even though legally Tiberius Claudius Nero was the father of Drusus, Octavian was suspected of being the real father. And he probably was!

These Imperial ties were further strengthened in A.D. 4 when Augustus adopted Tiberius—uncle of Claudius; and Tiberius, in turn, adopted Germanicus—brother of Claudius.

During the reigns of Augustus, Tiberius, and his nephew Caligula, Claudius was practically a nobody. When he wasn't drinking or gambling, he was reading and doing a little writing. He had a fondness for history. And then Caligula was assassinated. This changed everything!

When the assassins ordered the courtiers to disperse, Claudius hid behind a curtain. As he cringed in terror, a guard happened to notice his feet sticking out. The man jerked away the curtain, and then recognized Claudius. Thoroughly cowed, Claudius sank to the floor and grabbed the guard by the knees. He fully expected to be murdered on the spot.

But to his amazement, Claudius was told by the astonished man that the Guard wanted him to be Emperor! At this time, the Senate was thoroughly disgusted with the antics of the insane Caligula. Many of them believed that Rome should once again become a Republic. The Guard, however, demanded a monarchy—and so did the crowds choking the streets. And since Claudius was a "simpleton" anyway, the shrugging Senate let the military have its way.

Claudius showed his appreciation to the guard by presenting 15,000 sesterces to every member who had voted for him.

At the time of his election, Claudius was 50. Suetonius described him as being "tall, well-built, handsome, with a fine head of white hair and a firm neck, he stumbled as he walked owing to the weakness of his knees. . . . " (Will Durant suggests that at one time he had had polio.)

Often when he spoke, foam oozed from his mouth, and his nose ran. He suffered from gout, stuttered, and his head wobbled slightly as if it were attached to his shoulders by a spring. Also, he often fell asleep even when in public.

Having assumed the throne, he showed a generous spirit by offering amnesty to all who had agitated for a new constitution. Nevertheless he had the entire group of assassins who had murdered Caligula immediately put to death.

Claudius enjoyed sitting in judgment in court. Here, he liked to show what he considered to be his unusual wisdom. Once, when a woman along with a man appeared before him, there was a conflict as to whether or not the woman was the man's mother. Claudius solved the problem by requiring the woman to marry the man!

In another case in which the defendant was accused of posing as a Roman citizen, a dispute erupted as to whether the man should wear a Roman gown or a Greek mantle. Again Claudius solved the problem. His verdict was that he should wear the gown while he was being defended and the mantle when he was being accused.

Claudius was extremely susceptible to suggestion. Following the conviction of a man for forgery, the audience shouted, "He ought to have his hands cut off!" To this, Claudius responded immediately by asking that an executioner be brought with a block and cleaver.

The new emperor was devoted to his family line and liked to emphasize the greatness of his forebears. His most frequent oath was "By Augustus!" He persuaded the Senate to vote divine honors for his grandmother Livia, and he insisted that her image as well as the image of Augustus be driven around the Circus in an elephant-drawn carriage during the ritual procession preceding the games.

A passion for gambling stayed with Claudius throughout his life. And so thoroughly addicted was he, he had a special board for his carriage on which he could roll the dice without the dice falling off. Indeed, he loved throwing dice so much he wrote a book on the subject.

He was also attracted to gladiator shows; and when two combatants mortally wounded each other, he was so entranced he had their swords fashioned into pocketknives for his personal use. The flow of blood and human suffering excited him so much he decreed—says Suetonius—"that all combatants who fell accidentally should have their throats cut."

Whenever he could manage it, he liked to watch executions and the torture of prisoners. But so afraid was he of his own death that he was constantly surrounded with guards and "before entering a sickroom he always had it carefully gone over: pillows and mattresses were prodded, and bedclothes shaken out. Later, he even required all visitors to be searched when they came to pay him a morning call, and excused no one."

The marriages of Claudius were disasters. His first wife died on their wedding day. The next two were divorced. Then, at 48, he married Valeria Messalina who was a mere 16. Messalina was far from beautiful. She had a flat head, a deformed chest, and a florid face. Her second child was a boy named Tiberius Claudius who later came to be known as Britannicus in honor of the conquest of Britain which took place in A.D. 43 under the leadership of Claudius.

But Messalina was not satisfied in just being queen of the Roman Empire. Will Durant in *Caesar and Christ*, tells us that "she fell in love with the dancer Mnester; when he rejected her advances she begged her husband to bid him to be more obedient to her requests; Claudius complied, whereupon the dancer yielded to her patriotically." Thus helped by her husband, Messalina—spider fashion—lured many into her bed. Juvenal tells us that she even put on a disguise and worked in a brothel.

Eventually, after she had committed bigamy by marrying Caius Silius, Claudius ordered her death. He then solemnly announced that he would never remarry, and stated that if he did the Praetorian Guard was authorized to kill him. And yet, within a year, he began to plan for a new wife.

For a while Roman gossips were certain he would marry Lollia, an ex-wife of Caligula. Lollia was glamorous—and rich. She was frequently costumed in jewels valued at 40,000,000 sesterces (approximately $20,000,000 in 1982 currency). Lollia, however, could not compete with the wiles of Agrippina, daughter of Germanicus, brother of Claudius, and the elder Agrippina. As a niece of Claudius, she could be more familiar with the Emperor than others.

Few women in history—including Jezebel—have been as cunning and deceitful as Agrippina. Agrippina had lived in incest with her brother Caligula, and had been widowed twice. She had broken up the home of her sister-in-law in order to marry her last husband, Caius Crispus. Caius was extremely wealthy, and after he had made out his will in her favor, he mysteriously died. Many think Agrippina poisoned him. Now, with her vast inheritance, she was one of the wealthiest women in the world.

Agrippina had four brazen goals. She was determined to marry Claudius, get rid of his son and heir Britannicus, persuade Claudius to adopt her red-headed son Nero, and to make Nero heir to the Empire.

Following a well-planned program of hugging and kissing Claudius whenever she could, Agrippina broke down his defenses. Since such a marriage was plainly incestuous, and since the Emperor had already referred to his bride-to-be as "my daughter and foster-child, born and bred in my lap so to speak" (Suetonius), he was embarrassed. Still, he followed a clever way out. He persuaded a group of senators to insist that the marriage was in the public interest!

At the time of the wedding, Claudius was 57 while Agrippina was only 32. Extremely jealous, the new bride had Lollia executed because Claudius, in an unguarded moment, had made flattering remarks about her figure. Soon Agrippina had so much power she insisted that she share the imperial dais with her husband. Next, she persuaded Claudius to adopt her son Nero.

During his reign, Claudius relied heavily on three freedmen—Narcissus, Pallas, and Callistus. These former slaves held the top posts in government. Moreover, all three, through the acceptance of bribes and the sale of office, became some of the richest men of antiquity.

Pallas, formerly owned by Antonia, the mother of Claudius, was a favorite in the palace. Students of the New Testament are concerned with him, for he was a brother of Antonius Felix—procurator of Judea. It was before this former slave that Paul was tried (Acts 24:24,25).

Claudius was generally stern with corrupt officials. But he apparently never learned of the corruption and misrule of Felix because Pallas shielded him.

Josephus tells us that Felix was married three times, and that each wife was of royal blood. In addition, we are told that he had seduced each wife. At the time of the trial, he was married to Drusilla—daughter of Agrippa I and the former wife of the king of Emesa.

Felix, corrupt as he was, had a guilty conscience. Luke tells us, "And as he [Paul] reasoned of righteousness, temperance, and judgment to come, Felix trembled, and answered, Go thy way for this time; when I have a convenient season, I will call for thee" (Acts 24:25).

Luke also tells us about Felix's corruption, "He hoped also that money should have been given him of Paul, that he might loose him" (Acts 24:26). One wonders why Felix wanted a bribe from a poor man like Paul when his brother Pallas was estimated to be worth 300,000,000 sesterces (approximately $150,000,000 in 1982 currency).

The misrule of Felix in Judea can be seen by the fact that when the commander in Jerusalem decided to send Paul to Caesarea, 60 miles away, he had to take special precautions. Acts 23:14-24 tells the story. "See that you tell no man that you have revealed the plot to kill Paul," the commander told Paul's nephew as he sent him on his way. Paul's sister's son had sought out Paul to tell him that certain Jews were planning to kill him. Then the commander ordered a mount for Paul to ride and a bodyguard of 200 foot soldiers, 70 mounted horsemen, and 200 spearmen to assure the apostle's safe arrival to appear before Governor Felix!

That 470 men were required to deliver one prisoner to a city only a few miles away indicates that the Jews were rapidly arming themselves. Thus Felix was preparing for the outbreak of the Sicarii—Dagger-men—and the war that would erupt with the Romans in A.D. 66. (Members of these Dagger-men, also called Zealots, were pledged to kill all disloyal Jews.

Their usual method was to stab their victims from behind, and then disappear into the nearby crowd).

Although it is disputed, many believe that Christianity was being widely accepted among the Jews in Rome at this time. A note from Suetonius adds emphasis to this belief: "Because the Jews at Rome caused continuous disturbances at the instigation of Chrestus [Christ], he [Claudius] expelled them from the City."

Included with those who were expelled, was a couple, Aquila and Priscilla. Since these energetic Christians were tent-makers, they added Paul to their staff in Corinth, and they also were a great help to Apollos. Luke tells us, "They took him [Apollos] unto them, and expounded unto him the way of God more perfectly" (Acts 18:26). And thus, without knowing it, Claudius was a great help to Christianity.

Professor E. M. Blaiklock also thinks that Claudius may have made the first official reference to Christianity in a letter which he wrote in A.D. 41 to the people of Alexandria. Said Dr. Blaiklock: "There had recently been serious rioting between the Jewish and Gentile populations of the city, and Claudius addresses some sharp words of admonition to both parties. He tells the Jews that they must not invite illegal immigration into Alexandria of Jews from Syria or from other parts of Egypt, 'otherwise I will proceed against them with the utmost severity for fomenting a general plague which infests the whole world.' These final words so closely resemble language used elsewhere about Christianity (cf. Acts 24:5) that it has been suspected that the illegal immigrants from Syria might have been Christian missionaries" (The *Zondervan Pictorial Bible Atlas* edited by E. M. Blaiklock, 1969).

Claudius did not execute as many as did some of the other Roman emperors. But he accounted for his share. At least thirty-five senators and 300 knights lost their lives because of death warrants issued by him. Frequently forgetful, he sometimes ordered a man to be executed, forgot the order, and then wondered why the victim did not come to drink or roll dice with him.

In his spare time, this "stupid" man wrote books. His autobiography alone filled eight volumes; and his history of the Etruscans, written in Greek, filled another twenty. Thinking he could improve the Latin alphabet, he invented three new letters. One of these represented a vowel between u and i, and another took the place of the letters ps, and the third was a substitute for the consonantal form of v.

، So prolific was Claudius, the library in Alexandria had a special wing to house his works.

How could such a simpleton do so much literary work? Claudius answered this by claiming that he had merely pretended to be a fool in order to escape execution at the hands of Caligula. This explanation, however, does not satisfy historians. Perhaps the solution is that the world is apt to peg a man insane just because he does not accept the mores of his peers!

As Claudius aged, Agrippina exerted herself more and more. She sided with Pallas against Narcissus and had him condemned to a dungeon. She instituted a reign of terror and saw to it that the wealth of her victims was confiscated in order to bolster a depleted treasury. Deep in her heart was a fear that Claudius' son Britannicus would inherit the throne. She persuaded her husband to give his thirteen-year-old daughter Octavia to her sixteen-year-old Nero. Still she was afraid, for there was evidence that Claudius was beginning to see through her and that he was determined that Britannicus would be the new emperor.

Determined that this would never happen, Agrippina arranged for Claudius to be fed poisoned mushrooms. He died twelve hours later. He was in his sixty-fourth year.

Following a pompous funeral, the Senate voted him divine honors.

Chapter 8

They Call Him Nero

The shadows were lengthening across the warm hills of Rome as busy slaves erected final crosses in Nero's magnificent gardens. While they worked, soldiers brought in Christians and either tied them or nailed them to crosses. Next, they soaked them with inflammable pitch.

Darkness had frequently put a stop to the Emperor's chariot racing. This evening it would be different! The burning Christians would provide the light. Soon the chariots were lined up, the crosses were lit, and the horses leaped forward. As the clatter of the chariot wheels mingled, the crowds cheered. But there was no real enthusiasm in their cheers. Such flagrant cruelty was too much—even for them.

Seeing that he had displeased the crowd, Nero never repeated this performance. Instead, he contented himself by throwing Christians to the lions; by dressing them in animal skins and turning the dogs on them; and by killing those who were Roman citizens with the sword.

Today, Nero is remembered for his cruelties—and especially for having beheaded Paul. But strangely enough, in the beginning of his reign, he was immensely popular because of his generosity, kindness, and even understanding. Shortly after becoming Emperor at the age of seventeen, he was asked to sign a criminal's death warrant. As he faced the document, he cried out in genuine anguish, "Oh, why was I ever taught to write?"

While Claudius was dying on October 13, A.D. 54, Agrippina made certain that his death was kept secret until all arrangements had been finalized to place Nero on the throne. Nero, of course, was ecstatic at his elevation—even though he knew the truth. After divine honors had been voted for his stepfather, he remarked, "Mushrooms must be the food of the gods, since by eating them Claudius has become divine!"

Being an atheist, Nero thought his little joke exceptionally funny.

Nero's first speech to the Senate aroused great enthusiasm. "He set forth," wrote Tacitus, "the principles and models by following which he hoped to administer the affairs of the Empire in the best manner. . . . In his house, he said, there should be no bribery nor corruption, nor anything to the wiles of ambition, and his family concerns should be kept distinct from the affairs of state. . . . "

The senators so loved this message, they had it engraved on a pillar of solid silver and decreed that it should be read publicly once a year.

Blue-eyed, freckle-faced Nero had reddish-bronze hair and slightly heavy cheeks. He was the son of Gnaeus Domitius—a member of the Ahenobarbi family. For five hundred years this family, noted for its red beards, blue blood, recklessness and courage, had been at the top of Roman society. Nero's paternal grandfather was extravagant and had a passion for gladiatorial shows. Likewise, he was cruel to his slaves. Indeed, he was so cruel he was denounced by Augustus.

Nero's father was a profligate noted for incest, brutality, and adultery. He married Nero's mother when she was a mere thirteen. Dio quotes him as having said, "No good man can possibly come from us."

At his birth in A.D. 37 at Anzio, Nero was named Lucius

Domitius Ahenobarbus. He retained this name until his mother married Claudius. When he was adopted by his step-father his name was changed to Nero Claudius Drusus Germanicus.

The new emperor's boyish smile captivated almost everyone. But beneath that smile was an iron will. In the routine of things, he provided good government, grew slightly fat, raced his chariots, hired a voice teacher—and concentrated on singing.

Curiously, some of Nero's friends are well known to New Testament readers. His former tutor and current speech writer, Seneca, was the younger brother of Gallio who found Paul not "guilty of wrong or wicked lewdness," as recorded in Acts 18. And Vitellius, the senator who arranged with the Senate to legalize the marriage between his mother and Claudius, was a former governor of Syria. Indeed, it was he who dismissed Pontius Pilate. Also, Nero was the one who appointed Porcius Festus governor of Judea. Festus followed Felix and is one of the governors before whom Paul appeared (Acts 26:32).

Soon word filtered through to Nero that his mother was active in plots to take his life. At first he ignored these rumors and turned his attention onto Britannicus—his stepbrother and potent rival.

Finally, Nero decided that his stepbrother should die. Approaching his mother's old poison maker Locusta, he ordered a dose to be placed in Britannicus' drink. Alas, it merely acted as a laxative. He then summoned Locusta, and after personally flogging her, sneered, "So you think I'm afraid of the Julian laws against poisoning?"

He then pulled her into his bedroom and stood over her while she made a concoction he deemed strong enough. But unwilling to take a chance, he first tried it out on a goat. And since it took the goat five hours to die, he had her boil it down to make it stronger. Next, he tried it on a pig, and when the pig died immediately, Nero was ready.

NERO

That February, a banquet was arranged for some of the highborn young people. Among those who attended were Britannicus and Titus—the youth who later destroyed Jerusalem. In the midst of the festivities on that warm, sticky night, a waiter brought Britannicus a cup of hot wine. After diluting it with cold water, Britannicus took the fatal sup.

As servants carried the unconscious lad out of the banquet hall, Nero assured the guests that he had merely had an epileptic seizure. By the following dawn, Nero had the body cremated at Campus Martius. Little was said of the sudden death of the former emperor's son. Nero's fame continued to soar.

Now he became convinced that his mother was against him, that the rumors he had heard were true. He also decided that his only way out was to kill her. But how was he to do this without exciting public opinion? After long consideration, he decided that she should die by accident! He arranged for her to go home on a ship that was due to capsize.

The boat sank as planned, but Agrippina swam to safety; and since it was night, those who were in on the plot, did not notice her escape. Nero then selected three officers to do the job.

When a startled Agrippina viewed their swords, she jerked her skirt open and screamed, "Strike at the womb that bore Nero!"

With both his mother and Britannicus dead, Nero behaved like a famished tiger suddenly released from its cage. While in conversation, a friend quoted a famous line: "When I am dead, may fire consume the earth."

Placing a hand on the man's shoulder, Nero corrected him at once by saying, "While *I am yet alive*, may fire consume the earth." And he proceeded to do this with alacrity. He poisoned the aunt who had raised him, tore up her will, and seized her estate. Then he banished Octavia, the sister of Britannicus whom he had married when he was sixteen. Twelve days later he married his mistress, Poppaea. Later, he ordered Octavia to commit suicide.

In honor of his new wife, he began the construction of the enormous Golden House—one of the wonders of the empire. Set in vast gardens which included an artificial lake, he poured money into the new house with a lavish hand. Suetonius wrote: "Parts of the house were overlaid with gold and studded with precious stones. . . . All the dining rooms had ceilings of fretted ivory, the panels of which could slide back and let a rain of flowers, or of perfume from hidden sprinklers, shower upon his guests. The main dining room was circular, and its roof revolved slowly, day and night, in time with the sky. Sea water, or sulphur water, was always on tap in the baths. When the palace had been decorated throughout in this lavish style, Nero dedicated it and condescended to remark: 'Good, now I can at last begin to live as a human being!' "

In this palace he indulged in all kinds of vice and made no effort to keep it secret. There was a huge bath where Poppaea bathed in mare's milk for her complexion. There was a vomitorium where guests could tickle their throats with a feather, lose their dinners, and stagger back to gorge some more. (Ruins of this can still be seen.) The walls were covered with the finest paintings and tapestries. And in the corners and other prominent places there were fountains and statues.

From boyhood, Nero had loved horses, and now chariot racing became a passion. Those who raced with him, however, knew that it was expedient never to win! Upon returning home from the races one evening, Poppaea chided him mildly for being late. Enraged by her remark, he booted her in the stomach, and since she was pregnant, she died. Brokenhearted, Nero ordered a state funeral and built a temple in her honor. And it is said that he burned Syria's entire annual crop of incense at her side. But the incense did not restore her life.

Too soon Nero forgot Poppaea for a new passion. "Having found a youth, Sporus, who closely resembled Poppaea, he had him castrated, married him by a formal ceremony, and 'used him in every way like a woman'; whereupon a wit

expressed the wish that Nero's father had had such a wife"
(Will Durant in *Caesar and Christ*).

Nero's interest in the arts continued. He had a slender
talent. He began to write poetry, to paint—and especially to
sing. Soon he fancied that he was one of the world's truly great
singers. He entered into singing contests all over the Empire.
The prizes were always his—and he gloated over them. In
Athens, the audience gave him such an ovation he declared
that from then on Greece was to have dominion status. And at
this the audience cheered even more!

Nero had been reigning about ten years when suddenly on
July 19, A.D. 64, a fire broke out in Rome. The blaze started in
some wooden sheds just east of the Circus Maximus. Soon it
spread to the foot of the Palatine and Caelian Hills where vast
quantities of oil and other inflammables had been stored. In
those days the streets of Rome were very narrow and the
flames leaped from one house to the next.

The fire raged on for six days and as the buildings fell
thieves got busy looting, murdering, destroying.

When it seemed the conflagration had burned itself out, it
started again and burned for another three days. By the time
the fire was out, more than two-thirds of Rome was in ashes.
Nero was terribly shaken—especially because the libraries
and museums had been destroyed, He worked hard to take
care of the refugees. He erected a city of tents for them in the
Field of Mars, and brought in supplies of food for which he
paid out of his own pocket.

And then one sultry night he was seen on the tower of a garden theater across the Tiber where he had established his
headquarters. There was a lyre in his hands, and while the
crowd watched in horrified silence, he began to sing about the
sack of Troy while he accompanied himself on the lyre. Soon
word spread that Nero had set the fire. Such accusations were
even scrawled on public buildings. Nero became desperate for
a scapegoat to blame. Soon he found one.

In the words of Tacitus, he directed his fury against "a race of men detested for their evil practices, and commonly called Chrestiani. The name was derived from Chrestus who, in the reign of Tiberius, suffered under Pontius Pilate, Procurator of Judea. By that event the sect of which he was founder received a blow which for a time checked the growth of the dangerous superstition; but it revived soon after, and spread with recruited vigor not only in Judea . . . but even in the city of Rome, the common sink into which everything infamous and abominable flows like a torrent from all quarters of the world" (*Annals* 15:44).

With infinite cunning, Nero incited the Romans against the Christians. Tacitus wrote: "They were put to death with exquisite cruelty, and to their sufferings Nero added mockery and derision. . . . At length the brutality of these measures filled every breast with pity. Humanity relented in favor of the Christians."

After the debris had been cleared, Nero started to rebuild. Funds were called in from throughout the Empire and they were used to rebuild the homes of the citizens, and with no cost to them. Streets were widened and straightened. Water reservoirs were arranged so that another general fire could not take place—and the city was beautified. Indeed, such a fine job was done, enthusiasts wanted to change the name of the city from Rome to Nero!

Nero's fame leaped higher every day. The Senate even suggested starting the new year with December, the month of his birth, rather than the customary January. When he refused the honor, his popularity leaped even higher. Exaggerated stories were told about his kindness. It was said that when he learned of the illness of a friend, he sent all the way to Egypt for a doctor to treat him. It was also claimed that he wanted to eliminate indirect taxes throughout the Empire.

Soon Nero was confronted with a different type of trouble. During the winter of 65 and the spring of 66, plague broke out in Rome. Within weeks thirty thousand were dead and neither graves nor funeral pyres could be prepared fast enough. Many blamed Nero, saying that he had offended the gods.

Nero became extremely sensitive to criticism. Once "a comedian named Datus, who had to say the lines 'Goodbye, Father; goodbye, Mother!' in a play in which he was acting, pretended to be eating something which disagreed with him . . . (and he) made the motions of a swimmer, his reference being, of course, to the poisoned mushrooms given to Claudius and to the shipwreck of Agrippina. Nero banished him from the capital for his audacity." (*Nero* by Arthur Weigall. Garden City Publishing Co., 1930.)

From this point, his popularity plunged. The army revolted in Spain and Galba was declared the new emperor. The Senate now decreed that Nero was an outlaw. He fled from Rome in disguise. Cornered on a June evening, he crept into a basement, and there, shivering on a dirty cot, he tried to commit suicide. But the knife did not penetrate his throat deep enough; and so he begged his servant, Epaphroditus, to press the blade home. As he died, it is reported that he murmured, "What a great artist dies with me!" He was thirty-one and had ruled fourteen years.

By a remarkable coincidence, he died on June 9th, the anniversary of the date when he forced Octavia to commit suicide.

As we look at the grisly reign of Nero, we cannot help but remember that in the days of his greatest popularity Paul shivered in the Mamertine prison near the Forum. From this prison—if the Mamertine prison is the authentic one—it is quite possible that he could hear the cheers of the senators as they clapped and shouted their approval of Nero. But things have a way of reversing themselves. In our time the words of this curly-haired emperor are either forgotten or despised, while the epistles of Paul—many written in this very prison—are loved and quoted everywhere.

Today there is a common saying about these two contemporaries. That saying is this: "We name our sons Paul; but we name our dogs Nero!"

Chapter 9

Titus—He Crushed Jerusalem

Caligula's brazen announcement that he would have his statue erected in the Holy of Holies in Jerusalem filled the Jews with unspeakable horror. Nothing had stirred them so much since Antiochus Epiphanes had sacrificed a pig on the altar of the Temple. This was because erecting a statue was a direct violation of the commandment, "Thou shalt not make unto thee any graven image."

The Jews hoped that Caligula was merely teasing, for it was known throughout the Empire that he had a twisted sense of humor. But Little Boot was not teasing. He dispatched Petronius to Judea with an army along with orders to set up the statue even if it meant war.

Petronius invaded the country with two legions of Roman soldiers. Still, the Jews would not give in. They approached him by the tens of thousands and told him plainly that they would rather die than to have the statue erected. The bitter argument churned for months. Finally Petronius agreed that he would write to Rome and see if he could get the order changed. The moment he had finished speaking, a heavy, unexpected rain began to fall. And since it had not rained for a year, the Jews were confident that God was showing His approval to their resistance by ending the drought.

In Rome, Caligula's old friend, Herod Agrippa I, prepared a lavish dinner for the Emperor. Caligula was so pleased he told Agrippa that he should ask for a gift—any gift—and that he would bestow it. Agrippa then asked that his statue not be erected in the Temple. And although Little Boot was mildly shocked by the request, he agreed at once.

Having thus defied Rome and gotten away with it, the Jews—especially the Zealots—gripped their daggers in an even firmer grip and proceeded to defy their rulers in other matters. Unrest in the land continued to grow, and the blundering maleficence of Antonius Felix tended to bring this unrest to a climax. The breaking point came in May, A.D. 66, when the procurator, Florus, took seventeen talents from the Temple.

Some of the young people responded to this by carrying around baskets to gather money for the "poverty-stricken" ruler. This sarcasm infuriated Florus. He summoned his legions, looted hundreds of homes, and killed thousands. Many leading Jews were scourged and spiked to crosses. This slaughter ended in all-out war.

Joseph—now known as Josephus—was made the Jewish commander for all of Galilee. Nero responded by sending General Titus Flavius Vespasianus to lead the Roman legions. Square-jawed and nearly bald, Vespasian had distinguished himself in the conquest of Britain and thus seemed an ideal choice. Along with his son Titus he swooped down on Galilee from the north; and there, in the area where Jesus had preached, he won a stunning victory. He made six thousand slaves and sent them to Corinth to dig Nero's famous canal. Among the captives was Josephus.

By October, A.D. 67, all of Galilee had been subdued. In the summer of the next year, long before the rebellion was crushed, Nero committed suicide.

Nero's death was followed by chaos. While the war was still

raging in Judea, a message telling of Nero's death was sent to Servius Sulpicius Galba in Spain 332 miles away and it reached him in a record time of thirty-six hours. Upon arriving in Rome in June of 68, this former governor-general of Greater Germany, donned the purple.

Galba was addicted to most of the vices that afflicted his predecessors—including a passion for execution. Suetonius says: "He sentenced men of all ranks to death without trial on the scantiest of evidence, and seldom granted applications for Roman citizenship." Still, he ruled with some justice, and he had a passion for economy. He was far from well and could not wear shoes due to his misshapen feet, twisted and swollen by gout.

The leading politicians were unhappy because they could not freely dip into the treasury, thus his popularity soon ended. While marching to the Forum, the Guard intercepted him as he was being carried on a litter. Told that he must die, he thrust out his neck and his head was hacked off. Next, they sheared away his lips and chopped off his arms. A soldier then attempted to pick up the head by the hair. But since the hair was too slippery from blood, the soldier stuck his thumb into the mouth and carried the trophy to Otho as a symbol of his call to mount the throne.

Otho presented the blue-eyed trophy to a group of servants. These men placed it on the end of a spear and paraded with it around the camp chanting:

Galba, Galba, Cupid Galba,
Please enjoy your vigor still.

Galba's reign had lasted only six months.

Marcus Salvius Otho had been a senator. Bankrupt, he declared, "I might as well fall to some enemy as to my creditors in the Forum." He suggested that the only way he could square his accounts was by being made Emperor.

A sympathetic Senate—made even more sympathetic by bribery and conspiracy—complied. In the meantime the army in Germany hailed Quintus Vitellius—son of the governor of

Syria who had dismissed Pontius Pilate—Emperor. Vitellius had been a favorite at court, and had a certain earthy wisdom. After Caligula had declared that the moon-goddess had descended to embrace him, he inquired if Vitellius could see her. "No," the latter replied, "only you gods can see one another."

After several battles with Vitelius upon his invasion of Italy, Otho decided that his chance of survival was hopeless. Following a night with two daggers under his pillow, Otho plunged one of them into his side at dawn. At the time of his death he was thirty-five. His reign had lasted only ninety-five days.

At the news of Otho's death, Vitellius marched on Rome in full uniform and took the throne. Nero was his model and he started his reign by making a sacrifice to him. Vitellius was an accomplished glutton. He often gorged at three or four feasts in a single day. His taste was exotic and he craved such things as peacock brains, flamingo tongues, and pike livers.

Thoroughly disgusted with the performance of this man, Vespasian, while still battling in Judea, sent Antonius, one of his generals, to Italy in order to dethrone the "imposter." After one of the bloodiest battles in history, Antonius prevailed and entered Rome. Vitellius was dragged from his hiding place, and with a noose around his neck was pulled half naked through the streets of the city amidst the taunts of the crowd who called him such names as "greedy-guts." After he had been killed, his corpse was attached to a hook and dragged through a few more streets and then flung into the Tiber.

At the time of his death, Vitellius was fifty-six. There are conflicting reports as to the length of his reign. However, all are agreed that it was less than one year.

Before Vespasian hurried away to Rome to don the purple, he placed his son Titus in charge of the Jewish war.

The moon was riding high when Titus appeared before Jerusalem with 80,000 men. There were regular troops, engineers, and cavalry—and sprinkled among these veterans were many Arabs. At the time of his appearance, the Holy City was overflowing with devout pilgrims who had come to celebrate Passover.

As Titus appeared, a fierce civil war was going on behind the walls. Zealots and moderates were stabbing each other and the streets were turning crimson. When Titus demanded surrender, the Jews laughed with scorn and continued to hack at one another.

The Romans now drew siege engines to the northern wall and began operations. These engines—*scorpiones* and *ballistae*—were capable of tossing one-hundred-pound stones six hundred feet. As the stones thudded the walls, the factions within the city united to fight a common invader. Soon a large hole was smashed in the northern wall. Five days later the second wall was pierced and the dusty legions streamed through. Here a bloody hand-to-hand battle seesawed back and forth. Ultimately the northern section was in Roman hands.

Titus now decided on a new strategy—psychological warfare. He determined to frighten the city into submission. Accordingly, he issued orders for the men to don their smartest regalia, polish their shields and armor, and costume their horses with their brightest displays. Then he ordered them to solemnly march past while he doled out pay and rations. And so for four days the legions tramped by in full view of the Jews on the walls and behind spy holes.

But the Jews were not impressed!

Still thinking there must be an easy way to get Jerusalem to surrender, Titus sent Josephus—his former enemy—to plead with the people. He felt that the defeated commander of Galilee would have a special influence on his kinsmen. Josephus found a place on the wall where he was relatively safe from arrows, and began to beg the people to surrender. His long speech concluded with this paragraph: "O miserable creatures! are you so unmindful of those who used to assist you, that you will fight by your weapons and by your hands against the Romans? When did we ever conquer any other nation by such means? and when was it that God, who is creator of the Jewish people, did not avenge them when they had been injured?"

But the defenders were not ready to surrender. Titus then had ramps built and placed siege engines on top so that he could hurl boulders even further into the city. Failing with this method, he resolved to starve them out. A wall—*circumvallatio*—was built around the city. This nearly stopped the brave ones who had been slipping in and out in the darkness in order to get supplies.

Nevertheless, there were still desperate men who would do anything to escape the besieged city that was already filled with the stench of the dead and dying. Such men swallowed jewels and bits of gold, thus hoping to smuggle their treasure out. Few escaped. Greedy Roman soldiers hunted them down, ripped them open, and groped through their entrails for the valuables. Also, Titus ordered that anyone caught outside the city was to be crucified. Altogether, says Josephus, about five hundred were crucified every day. To find wood for the crosses and ramps, every tree in the area was cut down. Even the Mount of Olives was laid bare.

Still the Jews would not surrender!

Famine now came to the city with a vengeance. Death was everywhere. Josephus who was on the outside and whose family was on the inside recorded the events carefully. "Then did the famine widen its progress, and devoured people by whole houses, and families. . . . As for burying them, those that were sick themselves were not able to do it . . . the lanes of the city were filled with dead bodies. . . . A deep silence also, and a kind of deadly night, had seized the city; while yet the robbers were still more terrible than the miseries themselves; for they brake open the houses which were no other than the graves of the dead bodies, and plundered them of what they had. . . . Now everyone of these died with their eyes fixed on the Temple."

Cannibalism of the most flagrant kind was practiced.

Josephus records that even Titus was appalled. "However, when Titus, in going his rounds along these valleys, saw them full of dead bodies, and the thick putrefaction running about them, he gave a groan; and spread out his hands to heaven and called God to witness that this was not his doing."

Even as the people starved, battering rams were crashing into the walls. Finally, at the beginning of July, the Tower of Antonia—named in honor of Mark Antony—fell to the Romans. This tower stood close to the Temple. The soldiers were now anxious to capture this magnificent place of worship known throughout the Roman Empire as one of the wonders of the world. Some of the officers thought it would make an ideal fortress. But Titus opposed them. He did not want the Temple damaged.

However, in the heat of the battle, some of the legionnaires lost their heads. A soldier tossed a flaming torch through the Golden Window into the Holy of Holies. Filled with jars of holy oil and old paneling, the sacred room was soon an oven of flames.

Horrified, Titus ordered the fire quenched. But the men were not interested in putting it out, and perhaps even if they had been it would have been an impossibility.

Crazed by success, Titus went to unbelievable extremes. "Caesar ordered the whole city and the Temple to be razed to the ground. He left standing only the towers of Phasael, Hippicus, Mariamne, and a part of the wall on the west side." Josephus adds that 97,000 prisoners were taken and that 115,800 corpses were removed from the city. In that terrible month of August, A.D. 70, the Temple was destroyed and it has never been rebuilt, although Julian the Apostate made such an attempt during his short reign—A.D. 360-363.

Jerusalem with its 600,000 inhabitants had been humiliated.

Titus returned to Rome with his Jewish mistress, Bernice— sister of the King Agrippa before whom Paul made his appeal (Acts 25:23). With thousands of Jewish slaves in chains behind him, and with the spoils of victory in the hands of his men, he marched in triumph through the city on the Tiber.

An arch celebrating this triumph was then erected near the Forum, and even to this day it stands in excellent condition. Titus wanted to marry Bernice, but he was dissuaded by Vespasian. After the death of Vespasian's wife, he had lived in common law with a freedwoman, and following her death, with a number of concubines. And the Emperor felt that his son could do the same.

In A.D. 72, Vespasian started to build the huge Flavian Amphitheater—commonly known today as the Colosseum. The building which was designed to seat from 60-80,000 was 620 feet long and 513 feet wide. It was named in honor of the obscure Flavian family from which Vespasian was descended.

Seven years after the building had been started, Vespasian suddenly felt a spell of giddiness. "Alas, I think I am becoming a god," he said with his wry sense of humor. Then he struggled to his feet while he muttered, "An emperor should die standing." With these last words he passed away and Titus became the new emperor.

At the time of Vespasian's death, he was nearly seventy.

With the help of thousands of Jewish slaves, Titus finished the Flavian Amphitheater where so many thousands of Christians were to be martyred. The dedication took place in A.D. 80, and Titus decreed that the dedicatorial celebrations should last 100 days.

During the period of dedication, five thousand animals lost their lives. Lions were pitted against elephants, bears against bulls, and, alas, men against men.

Nothing seemed to please the people more than a cataract of blood. Perhaps Titus was inspired by the butchery in Jerusalem during his most glorious days. He passed away in his forty-second year while visiting the same house in which his father had died. His rule had lasted only a little more than two years and two months. Pious Jews said that he suffered an early death because he had desecrated the Holy of Holies.

What happened to the Jerusalem Christians during this terrible time? Eusebius, the first church historian (A.D. 260?-340), says: "Furthermore, the members of the Jerusalem church, by means of an oracle given by revelation to acceptable persons there, were ordered to leave the City before the war began and settle down in a town in Peraea called Pella" (*The History of the Church* by Eusebius, Penguin Classics).

If John Mark, as many scholars believe, wrote the Gospel that bears his name in this period, it is significant that one will find no bitterness in his book concerning the destruction of Jerusalem. This lack of bitterness is all the more remarkable when we remember that strong tradition says that Mark's mother owned considerable property within the city. The solution is that John Mark had found the *Other City* and was quite satisfied.

The loss of property is not catastrophic to those who know Christ!

Chapter 10

Domitian—He Exiled John

Among the many Roman emperors whose fingers were smudged with the blood of Christians was Domitian, son of Vespasian, and younger brother of Titus. He was the last of the Flavians.

Second only to Nero in cruelty in this period, Domitian's proscriptions included members of his own family. Included within his boodthirsty goals was a determination to execute all descendants of King David's line. And numbered with these, according to Eusebius, were the grandsons of Jude—brother of Jesus.

Unfortunately we do not have the names of many of Domitian's victims. But this sinister fact adds even more grimness to the horror of his tyranny. The names were not recorded for the obvious reason that Christians were considered far too insignificant to have their names written down. To Domitian, murdering a Christian was like swatting a fly.

One of his would-be victims, however, is known. Early Christian writers assure us that it was Domitian who persecuted John the Revelator. At first he had him arrested in Ephesus where he was doing a mighty work in the church.

Then he brought him to Rome and had him tossed into a cauldron of boiling oil that seethed and bubbled in front of the Latin Gate.

Having escaped death from the oil by a miracle, John was banished as a slave to the stone quarries on the Isle of Patmos. It was there he had his colorful visions and wrote the book known as The Revelation of St. John the Divine.

As was generally the case, the problem that wedged itself between Domitian and the Christians was that of the Emperor's self-deification. The Christians, as Paul had admonished in Romans thirteen, tried to obey him as their ruler, but they absolutely refused to worship him—even though that worship entailed the mere burning of a few grains of incense. And this was an extremely sore point, for Domitian stubbornly insisted that he was divine. After he took back his divorced wife Domitia, he referred to his action as "a recall to my divine bed." Also, he encouraged the masses to cheer him and his wife in the Colosseum with the shout, "Long live our Lord and Lady!"

In a brazen letter to the Senate, Domitian began with the words: "Our Lord God instructs you to do this." Indeed, he insisted that he was not just a god, but God! He even went so far as to rule that whenever he was referred to in documents, he was to be mentioned as *Dominus et Deus Noster*—Our Lord and God."

Such stark blasphemy was too much for the Christians— and the Jews. Yes, even the Romans shuddered!

From the time of Domitian's birth on October 24, A.D. 51 in Rome's Pomegranate Street, conflicts began to writhe and lash within his mind. His brother Titus was ten years older and as the heir-apparent, received most of the attention. During official parades, Titus rode up front with Vespasian seated in a coveted curule chair while Domitian tagged behind in a litter.

This rivalry between himself and his brother increased with the years. And it was given a decided boost when Titus returned to Rome for a hero's welcome after destroying Jerusalem. In the gala parade that swept through the important avenues, Titus and his father were given most of the credit.

When Titus ascended the throne at the time of Vespasian's death, Domitian declared that his father's will had been altered and that he should have shared the Empire. Titus offered to share power with him, but Domitian angrily refused the offer. Instead, he began to plot both privately and openly. One of his plots, unashamedly designed to gather public approval, was "offering his troops twice as large a bounty as Titus had offered them." He also planned military conquests in which he could shine.

But events changed sooner than Domitian had dared to hope. Titus fell seriously ill. Domitian rushed to his bedside and one way or another quickened his death. One source has it that he covered him with snow. Suetonius claimed that he "told the attendants to presume his death by leaving the sickbed before he had actually breathed his last."

In this manner, Domitian ascended the throne.

Domitian is remembered as a vain and lazy man. He had a ruddy complexion, was tall and strong, had large moon-like eyes, and was exceedingly proud of his hair. As a matter of fact, he was so proud of his hair, he wrote a book entitled *Care of the Hair*. But as often happens, he soon lost his hair, developed a paunch, and his once solid legs became thin and spindly with hammer-like toes.

Upon assuming power, Domitian tried to get the Empire to forget Titus as soon as possible. Whenever he was forced to refer to him, he did so indirectly. Nevertheless, probably because of public opinion, Domitian was compelled to complete the Arch of Titus raised in memory of his brother's victory over the Jews.

Having become Emperor, Domitian seemed bored with his work. In the early days, it is said that he spent much of his time catching flies. He liked to spear them with a pen. When an

important visitor asked if someone was with the Emperor,
Vivius Crispus is alleged to have replied: "No, not even a fly."
This story became one of the behind-the-hand jokes of the
time.

Like Nero and others, Domitian tried to rule with moderation and justice—in the beginning. During those first years he
attempted to stamp out immorality. An unchaste Vestal Virgin
was executed. He outlawed the making of eunuchs and
lowered their price on the slave market in order to discourage
the practice. He stopped the ritual sacrifice of oxen and
outlawed indecent pantomime. He even refused legacies if it
could be shown that they would impoverish the children.

Thinking the Empire needed the steadying influence of
religion, Domitian set out to encourage the old Roman faiths.
During the great fires of 79 and 82, the Temple of Jupiter,
Juno, and Minerva had been destroyed. He ordered this Temple rebuilt and lavished it with gold plated doors and a gilded
roof. The new building cost over 50,000,000 sesterces—an
amount that caused the Senate to wince.

Domitian encouraged sculpture, poetry, and music. He even
wrote poetry himself. He rebuilt libraries and searched the
Empire for the finest volumes. Indeed, he ruled with creative
ability for several years. Then, like Nero and Caligula, he
became drunk with power. A cruel and haughty spirit completely possessed him. He altered his name to Germanicus
and then renamed the months of September and October to
Germanicus and Domitianus. The reason? He was born in
October and became Emperor in September!

He decreed that images of himself be placed throughout the
city and that those in more prominent places be made of silver
or gold. He even stipulated the minimum weight of the precious metal.

With uncontrolled arrogance, Domitian became so suspicious of others he ordered executions at the slightest cause.
Offended by some allusions in an historical work of Hermogenes
of Tarsus, he ordered him put to death and had the slaves who

had copied the work crucified. One person was killed because he insisted on celebrating the birthday of his uncle, the former emperor Otho. Another was put to death merely because he resembled a man Domitian hated.

Executing people became a sport, as did all kinds of torture. One of the tortures Domitian developed was that of scorching a victim's genitals. Once he invited a man to dine with him even though he had secretly ordered his crucifixion on the following day. All of this, of course, made Domitian fear for his own life. This fear soon became such an obsession he had the place where he took his daily walk lined with mirrors. Thus he was able to glance in several directions and avoid assassination.

Since both Domitian's father and brother had been in Jerusalem, he had undoubtedly heard of the Jewish belief in the coming of the Messiah, and he had also heard of the second coming of Jesus Christ. These beliefs frightened him, and like Herod the Great, he decided to do something about it. Many Christians who refused to burn incense to Domitian were liquidated. Among these was his own nephew Flavius Clemens.

Through Jewish prophecy, he learned that the Messiah was to be from the descendants of David. He therefore decided that he would eliminate all these descendants. Because of this determination, he arrested the grandsons of Jude. As he faced them, he demanded to know how much money they possessed. The men replied that they had a mere twenty-five acres between them. Holding up calloused hands, they explained how difficult it was to scratch a living from their unproductive soil. Impressed with their seeming honesty, Domitian began to inquire about Jesus and His kingdom.

"When asked about Christ and his kingdom—what it was like, and where it would appear—they explained that it was not of this world or anywhere on earth but angelic and in heaven, and would be established at the end of the world, when he would come in glory to judge the quick and the dead. . . .

On hearing this, Domitian found no fault with them, but despising them as beneath his notice let them go free and issued orders terminating the persecution of the Church. On their release they became leaders of the churches, both because they had borne testimony and because they were of the Lord's family; and thanks to the establishment of peace they lived on into Trajan's time" (*The History of the Church* by Eusebius).

Thus miraculously, thousands were spared.

But although Domitian stopped persecuting Christians, he continued his tyranny. In 96 he suddenly became suspicious of his secretary Epaphroditus. Casting about for an excuse to execute him, he remembered that Epaphroditus had helped Nero commit suicide twenty-seven years before. (This Epaphroditus is alleged to have been a convert to Judaism; thus he was not the man who took the gift to Paul from the Philippian Church.) Because of this, he had him killed. This so frightened the other workers in Domitian's household, they decided to assassinate him. Domitian's wife, Domitia, joined the conspiracy.

At the agreed time, the servants burst into the royal bedroom and after a brief skirmish the man who had ruled for fifteen years was dead. When the Senate learned of his death, they ordered all his statues destroyed and all the inscriptions mentioning him defaced.

And thus it was that the man who considered himself to be God, and who demanded that the world worship him, was killed by his own wife and a few servants. At the time of his death, September 18, A.D. 96, he had ruled fourteen years. He was only forty-four.

Domitian was denied a public funeral.

Chapter 11

That Famous Trajan Letter

Following the death of Domitian, Nerva, considered one of the *five good emperors*—the list also includes, Trajan Hadrian, Antoninus Pius, and Marcus Aurelius—ascended the throne at the age of sixty-six. Nerva recalled many of Domitian's exiles, lowered taxes, and put a stop to executions.

But the Praetorian Guard did not like him. His economies cramped their style, and so they stormed the palace. Without resisting, Nerva offered them his throat. Miraculously, however, they spared him on condition that he adopt a son to follow him who would be acceptable to both the Senate and the Guard.

Nerva adopted Marcus Ulpius Trajanus—known today as Trajan. And after a rule of only sixteen months, Nerva was replaced by Trajan. Trajan was heading a Roman army in Cologne at the time of his election. But instead of rushing to Rome to enjoy the honor, he remained at his post for nearly two years in order to complete some projects he had started. This was characteristic of his way of doing things.

This tall, handsome man is remembered today for many things. He was a great builder, an able and hard-working administrator, had the courage of a lion, and was generally a man of simple tastes. In addition, his troops loved him. But oddly enough, Christendom's memories of Trajan do not center around these things.

Instead, he is remembered best for a letter—a letter which he probably dashed off in a few minutes without too much thought.

The reason this letter is so famous is because it is the first official letter from a Roman Emperor which specifically names and concerns itself with Christians. (In the letter of Claudius mentioned previously, it is merely *assumed* that he was referring to Christians. Also, they are not identified.) This letter— found in Paris in 1500—is in regard to the martyrdom of Christians. And among those who died as a result of this correspondence was the revered Polycarp, Bishop of Smyrna.

Pliny—nephew and adopted son of Pliny the Elder—had been sent to Bithynia as *corrector civitatium* and was answerable to Trajan. By this time Christianity was becoming known as something more than just a sect in Judaism. Also, it was spreading rapidly. In Asia Minor there were churches at Ephesus, Colossae, Laodicea, Hierapolis, Sardis, Pergamum, Smyrna, Philadelphia—and other places. This new faith presented a problem he did not understand. And being a lawyer by profession, Pliny was anxious to do everything in a legal way.

A basic tenet of Roman rule was not to interfere with the religious beliefs of its subjects. Thus the Jews were not forced to eat pork and they were allowed to practice circumcision. There were, of course, emperors who violated this law.

There was a time when the emperors could merely shrug at Christianity. But that time had ended. Upon taking his position in Bithynia, Pliny learned that Christianity was a force in that area. Peter's first epistle was addressed to the Jewish Christians "scattered throughout Pontus ... and Bithynia" (I Peter 1:1). Also Luke, the New Testament's prolific author, had died—probably by hanging—in Bithynia. Puzzled about what he should do, Pliny sought the advice of Trajan. After greetings and assurances of loyalty, he wrote:

"I am unacquainted as to the method and limits to be observed in examining and punishing them. Whether, therefore, any difference is to be made with respect to age . . . between the young and the adult; whether repentance admits to pardon; or if a man has once been a Christian, it avails him nothing to recant; whether the mere profession of Christianity, albeit without any criminal act, or only the crimes associated therewith are punishable; in all these points I am greatly doubtful.

"In the meantime the method I have observed toward those who have been denounced to me as Christians, is this: I interrogated them whether they were Christians; if they confessed I repeated the question twice again, adding a threat of capital punishment; if they still persevered, I ordered them to be executed; for I was persuaded, that whatever the nature of their creed, a contumacious and inflexible obstinacy certainly deserved chastisement. There were others also brought before me possessed with the same infatuation: but being citizens of Rome, I directed them to be carried thither.

"These accusations, from the mere fact that the matter was being investigated, began to spread, and several forms of mischief came to light. A placard was posted up without any signature, accusing a number of people by name. Those who denied that they were Christians, or had ever been so, who repeated after me an invocation to the gods, and offered religious rites with wine and frankincense to your statue (which I had ordered to be brought for the purpose, together with those of the gods), and finally cursed the name of Christ (none of which, it is said, those who are really Christians can be forced into performing), I thought proper to discharge. Others who were named by the informer at first confessed themselves Christians, and then denied it; true, they had been of that persuasion formerly, but had now quitted it (some three years, others many years, and a few as much as twenty-five years ago). They all worshipped your statue and the images of the gods, and cursed the name of Christ.

"They affirmed, however, that the whole of their guilt or their error was, that they met on a certain fixed day before it was light and sang an antiphonal chant to Christ, as to a god, binding themselves by a solemn oath, not to any wicked deeds, but to never commit any fraud, theft or adultery, never to falsify their word, nor deny a trust when they should be called upon to deliver it up; after which it was their custom to separate, and then reassemble to partake of food—food of an ordinary innocent kind. . . .

"I therefore thought it proper to adjourn all further proceedings in this affair, in order to consult with you. For the matter is well worth referring to you, especially considering the numbers endangered: persons of all ranks and ages, and of both sexes, are and will be involved in the prosecution. For this contagious superstition is not confined to the cities only, but has spread through the villages and countryside. Nevertheless it seems still possible to check and cure it. . . . " (*Private Letters, Pagan and Christian*, compiled by Dorothy Brooke, E. P. Dutton & Co., 1930).

Trajan replied:

"The method you have pursued, my dear Pliny, in sifting the cases of those denounced to you as Christians is eminently proper. . . . *No search should be made for these people* [italics mine]; when they are denounced and found guilty they should be punished; but when the accused party denies that he is a Christian, and gives proof . . . by adoring our gods, he shall be pardoned. . . . Information without the accuser's name subscribed shall not be admitted in evidence against anyone" (*Pliny the Younger, Letters*, Loeb Library).

This policy of not prosecuting Christians unless they were accused was generally followed during Trajan's reign. But although he did not instigate wholesale persecutions as did Nero, he did execute many. Among his victims were Ignatius, Bishop of Antioch; and Cleophas, a reputed cousin of the Lord Jesus Christ.

Trajan soon tired of administrative work. War was the passion of his life. Following two long Dacian campaigns, he turned his legions to the East. He overran Armenia and northern Mesopotamia and added these countries to his Empire. Then, exalted by success, he continued on down the Tigris River to the Persian Gulf. Stooped by age and fatigue, he longed for the youth of Alexander the Great.

Soon enemies on both sides began to attack. He lost much of what he had conquered. But with a mighty effort he gained some of it back. Then, while in the midst of grandiose plans, he was stricken by dropsy. This was followed by a stroke. Unable to go on, he was carried toward the Cilician coast. From here, he hoped to sail for Rome.

In the City-on-the-Tiber, the Senate was preparing a welcome that would rival the welcome given to the great Augustus. But, alas, Trajan died at Selinus while on the way in A.D. 117. He was sixty-four. He was cremated and his ashes sent to Rome where they were buried beneath the famous column he had created. However, no trace of the ashes has ever been uncovered.

At the time of his death, Trajan had no idea that he would be remembered best because of a letter he had directed against the hated Christians. In his eyes, followers of Christ were too insignificant to even notice!

Chapter 12

Bar-Kokhba
—the Accepted Messiah

Until recently, the name Bar-Kokhba was either not in the typical Bible dictionary, or it appeared merely as a footnote. With what we know today, this is amazing, for as the leader of the Second Revolt Bar-Kokhba is one of the most colorful personalities in the Christian era. Indeed, he was so colorful many leading rabbis accepted him as the Messiah! Why then, have we known so little about him?

The main answer to that question is that there was no Josephus to record the events of the Second Revolt, as he recorded the events of the First Revolt—the one crushed by Titus.

But today, thanks to archaeology, all of this is changed. One evening in 1960, Prime Minister David Ben-Gurion, Cabinet ministers, and members of the Israeli Knesset, with others, met in the home of President Ben Zvi in Jerusalem. Suddenly, as he was flashing pictures on a screen, noted archaeologist Yigael Yadin turned to the President of Israel and said: "Your Excellency, I am honored to be able to tell you that we have discovered fifteen despatches written or dictated by the last President of Israel 1800 years ago" (*Bar-Kokhba* by Yigael

Yadin, Random House, 1971).

This shattering announcement was followed by absolute silence. And then cries of astonishment and joy shook the room. On the following day banner headlines appeared throughout the world.

Since the Jews had been so thoroughly defeated by the Romans in A.D. 70, and since their Temple, the very center of their life and devotion, had been utterly destroyed, it seemed they and their religion were finished forever. But encouraged by their rabbis, and prodded by their gloating conquerors whose bad taste inspired them to issue a coin with *Judaea Capta* inscribed on it, Judaism kept squirming for a new birth.

In A.D. 115 a revolt erupted in Cyrenaica. This was followed by rebellion in Mesopotamia a year later. Thoroughly alarmed, the Romans strangled the uprising through the leadership of a Romanized Moor by the name of L. Quietus. Again, Jewish resistance was brought under control, but it was not eliminated.

Friction between the Jews and Romans continued to increase. And this friction burst into flames when Hadrian extended Domitian's law against castration to include circumcision. This law stirred the Jews to their very depths.

Then in A.D. 132 Simeon Bar-Kokhba made his appearance.

For centuries, Bar-Kokhba has been a semi-real Robin Hood type of hero to Jews all over the world. This is true even though references to him in ancient literature have been few and inconclusive. For centuries in Eastern Europe the Jewish holiday Lag B'Omer, commemorating the scholars, has been accompanied by special games staged in the fields by the children. In these games, the children arm themselves and pretend they are either Bar-Kokhba or his Roman enemies.

But today, thanks to the archaeologists, we know that Bar-Kokhba was a real man. And we also know, as Yigael Yadin showed with his slides, that he was the president of an independent Israel.

By A.D. 132, Bar-Kokhba had gathered an army sufficiently strong to lash out against the Romans. His main problem had been that of arming his men. This he solved by a clever but dishonest ruse. He arranged for his leaders to acquire the rights to supply weapons to the Roman commanders. By design, many of these weapons were of inferior quality. When they were rejected, they were hidden in strategic caves to be ready for the rebellion.

Possessing a magnetic personality, Bar-Kokhba was accepted as the Messiah by many. And among those who felt this way about him was the brilliant Akiba. Concerning this man, a modern Jewish writer has said: "Akiba, who followed Gamaliel, is one of the most famous Jews of all times. Starting late in life he became the most learned of his fellow rabbis. He was especially expert at basing new rules and decisions on words and passages in the Bible. He was known for his defence of the weaker members of society. . . . " (*The Eternal People* by Charry and Segal, United Synagogue of America, 1967).

Akiba was thoroughly impressed with Bar-Kokhba; and since that name means *Son of a Star*, Akiba connected him with the prophecy of Numbers 24:17—"There shall come a Star out of Jacob, and a Sceptre shall rise out of Israel, and shall smite the corners of Moab. . . ." He even went on to say of Bar-Kokhba: *"This is the King Messiah!"*

Bar-Kokhba was an excellent military strategist and disciplinarian. He demanded absolute obedience. Jewish sources claim that he even hacked off the fingers of his followers. When the wise ones asked, "How long will you continue to make the men of Israel blemished?" he answered, "How else shall they be tested?" Impressed, the sages answered, "Let anyone who cannot uproot a cedar from Lebanon be refused enrollment in your army."

These extreme statements may not be completely true, but there is no doubt that his army—estimated to have numbered 400,000—was an extremely tough army. Bar-Kokhba and his followers also brimmed with confidence. Some records indicate that they were almost blasphemous. "When they went forth to battle, they cried: (O God) neither help us nor disgrace us." This arrogance is surprising, for the items found in the caves which they had hidden indicate that they were devout followers of the Law.

In the beginning of the revolt, Hadrian seemed confident that it would be crushed with minimum effort. The Emperor was mistaken. Bar-Kokhba wiped out an entire Roman legion. And more humiliating still, this legion was the proud Twenty-second Deioterana—determined veterans from Egypt.

Victory after victory followed this Roman defeat. Soon Jerusalem was once again in the hands of the Jews. Animal sacrifices were restored and Bar-Kokhba was proclaimed the leader. Soon he began to issue his own coins, and the inscriptions on coins that have been found indicate his progress.

Stamped on one coin are the words: *Year One of the Redemption of Israel.* On another: *Year Two of the Freedom of Israel.* And yet another has the facade of the Temple with a star above it and the word *Jerusalem* by the side.

Some of the discovered orders of Bar-Kokhba indicate that he was either arrogant because of victory or desperate because of defeat. One order reads: *I take heaven to witness against me that unless you destroy the Galileans who are with you every man, I will put fetters on your feet as I did to ben Aphul.*

During these days of triumph, Eleazar became the High Priest, and Akiba was named the leader of the Sanhedrin.

The Christians had nothing to do with Bar-Kokhba. And perhaps the reason was that they remembered the words of Jesus: "If any man shall say unto you, Lo, here is Christ, or there; believe it not. For there shall arise false Christs . . . and shall shew great signs and wonders; insomuch that, if it were possible, they shall deceive the very elect. . . . Wherefore if they shall say unto you, Behold, he is in the desert; go not forth" (Matthew 24:23-26).

And since the Christians would not help him, Bar-Kokhba persecuted them. Eusebius wrote: "In the recent Jewish War, Bar-Kokhba, leader of the Jewish insurrection, ordered the Christians alone to be sentenced to terrible punishments if they did not deny Jesus Christ and blaspheme him."

When Hadrian realized that he was dealing with a military genius, he summoned Julius Severus from his post as governor of Britain and ordered him to end the revolt. Severus realized that he did not know the land with the thoroughness of the Jews and therefore he avoided pitched battles. Instead, he resorted to siege and the cutting of food supplies.

But even with the might of Rome it took three years to crush the rebellion. The price was appalling. Normally after a victory, the Emperor began his report to the Senate with the words: "If you and your children are in health, it is well; and the legions are in health. " But on this occasion, Hadrian omitted the words, *mihi et legionibus bene.*

The Romans, however, did not neglect vengeance. Nearly one thousand Jewish settlements and cities were destroyed, and 580,000 Jews lost their lives. Bar-Kokhba himself was killed by a Samaritan who then cut off his head and sent it to Hadrian.

Fragments of ancient scrolls—some of them doubtful— attribute all kinds of atrocities to the Romans. One of these states that they rolled Jewish children in holy books and then burned them. In addition, the city of Jerusalem was utterly destroyed. But more of that in the next chapter.

What happened to Bar-Kokhba? Even before he was killed, the people began to lose confidence in him. Some even whispered that his real name was *Bar-Coziba* (Son of Falsehood)!

Chapter 13

Hadrian
—He Renamed Jerusalem

From the time Jerusalem became a Jewish city thousands of years ago, Jews have revered it with a love that is almost unbelievable. The city has meant more to them than life. Indeed, it has meant so much, European Jew-baiters from the Middle Ages on through the days of Hitler have taunted them by shouting *Hep! Hep!*

That seemingly harmless syllable is made from the first letters of the Latin sentence *Hierosolyma est perdita* which means Jerusalem is lost. Such an idea to a Jew is unthinkable. And perhaps because of this confidence, tyrants have again and again sought to hurt the Jews by destroying Jerusalem.

As we have seen, Roman Emperor Titus burned the Temple and razed most of the city in A.D. 70. This is an event the Jews are determined never to forget. And even in our time, in order to remind themselves of that event, a Jewish bridegroom crushes a wineglass beneath his heel in the midst of his wedding ceremony.

Following the destruction of the city in A.D. 70, the Xth

Legion was left to control the ruins. The catastrophe of A.D. 135, however, was much more severe. Having defeated Bar-Kokhba, Roman Emperor Hadrian decided to destroy the city forever. His order was that the city should be plowed over and rebuilt—on Roman lines. And this was just the beginning of the insults that were heaped on the Jews.

The despised figure of a pig was carved over one of the gates in honor of the Xth Legion which had wrecked the city under Titus, a temple to Jupiter Capitolinus was erected at the site of Solomon's Temple, and the statue of Hadrian was stood at the spot once occupied by the Holy of Holies.

The new city received the name Aelia Capitolina. The Aelia glorified the name of the Emperor—Publius Aelius Hadrianus; and the Capitolina was in honor of Capitoline Jupiter—the new patron god of Rome.

All Jews were forbidden to enter the city, and any Jew who did was immediately crucified. An exception to this rule was made on the ninth day of Ab each year. This was the day the Temple was destroyed. By paying a fee, a Jew was allowed to enter in order to pray for the restoration of the Temple.

Both circumcision and the study of the Law were forbidden. However, Jews converted to Christianity were welcome in the city. But each male who sought admittance could be challenged to show that he had not been circumcised.

Tens of thousands of slaves were taken and shipped to Rome; and since such a vast number flooded the market, the price of a slave fell so low that it was cheaper to buy a slave than a horse. As a matter of record, there was such a large supply of slaves that many were freed. It was too expensive to feed them while awaiting a buyer.

In renaming and rebuilding Jerusalem, Hadrian sought to stamp out Judaism forever. But as often happens, the evil he intended accomplished a certain amount of good. Indeed, three historic blessings can be attributed to his misdeeds.

1. To divide Jerusalem into sections, two long colonnaded streets were laid out in such a way they crossed in the very

HADRIAN

center of the city. Thus, they formed the sign of the cross. This
fact caused comment for many a century. Some saw in this the
eternal truth that the cross can never be destroyed; others that
it supersedes the Mosaic Law.

2. One of Hadrian's motives was to stamp out all sacred
places in Jerusalem. To do this, he sought to obliterate them
by erecting pagan shrines on the same sites. But in doing so,
he merely marked the spots for future generations. Thus, his
pagan shrines identified the ancient location of the Temple
and other such renowned places.

3. Until Hadrian's time, Christianity was considered by the
uninformed to be merely a sect of Judaism. Then, due to Hadrian's
edict about Jews entering the city, the division between the
two was clearly indicated. For by affirming that they were not
followers of Judaism, Christians were allowed access to
the city.

As a final blow to the Jews, Hadrian renamed the province
of Judea. His new name was Palestina, in honor of the Philistines! (Actually, Hadrian merely legalized this name for it had
been used before, by Herodotus in the fifth century B.C.).

Today, not much can be seen of the ruins of Aelia
Capitolina. But archaeologists have been able to trace its
approximate setting, and occasionally a piece of tile or fragment of a drain shows up. The main north gate of the Roman
city was the Damascus Gate. This is known because of an
inscription of Herod Agrippa just above the gateway.

The inside story of how Hadrian became emperor may
never be known. Roman gossip had it that since Trajan died
without a natural heir, his widow Plotina managed to get
Hadrian onto the throne because she was in love with him.
Both Hadrian and Plotina denied this, but the story remained
in circulation during his entire reign. Forty-one-year-old
Hadrian was, however, Trajan's second cousin and nearest
relative. At the time of his election, he was governor of Syria
and was living in Antioch.

Hadrian was tall, elegant, and physically strong. Also, he

made beards popular by growing one himself. He loved the arts, wrote several books including an autobiography, painted, and was a fair sculptor. But his main passion was to build walls and new cities. And because of this building mania he even built tombs for his beloved dogs.

Hadrian was born in Italy. But then his family moved to Spain. Perhaps it was this that interested him in travel. And because he was a talented administrator, he was able to be away from Rome for as much as five years at a time. As he traveled, he always traveled with experts. In England, he marked one of his frontiers by a wall. Some of the ruins of this wall still remain. This mighty Hadrian Wall was seventy-three miles long, ten feet thick at the base, and twenty feet high. It was also completely fortified.

While in Athens, he was appalled at the lack of employment, and so he began to construct magnificent new buildings. These buildings, designed in the finest Greek fashion, included libraries, temples, and gymnasiums. He also threaded the country with aqueducts. By the time he left, Athens was probably the most beautiful city in the Empire.

Hadrian was superstitious and promoted the old Roman faiths. Actually, however, he had little personal concern with religion. But he is remembered for a letter which in essence was a breakthrough for Christians. Wrote Hadrian:

"To Minucius Fundanus. I have received a letter written to me by His Excellency Serennius Granianus, your predecessor. It is not my intention to leave the matter uninvestigated, for fear of causing the men embarrassment and abetting the informers in their mischiefmaking. If then the provincials can so clearly establish their case against the Christians that they can sustain it in a court of law, let them resort to this procedure only, and not rely on petitions and mere clamor. Much the most satisfactory course, if anyone should wish to prosecute, is for you to decide the matter. So if someone prosecutes them and proves them guilty of any illegality, you must pronounce sentence according to the seriousness of the offence. *But if anyone starts such proceedings in the hope of financial reward, then for goodness sake arrest him for his shabby trick, and see that he gets his deserts.*" (Italics added. *History of the Church* by Eusebius.)

One wonders what would have happened to Judas Iscariot if this law had been in effect at the time he identified Jesus for thirty pieces of silver!

Hadrian, in spite of his slaughter of the Jews, was concerned with law and mercy. Thus, historians include him as one of the "five good emperors." Once when he told a woman that he didn't have time to listen to her case, she replied: "Don't be an emperor, then." And instead of having her executed, as would have many another emperor, he listened to her problems.

Soon after the Jewish war, Hadrian was stricken with a disease that resembled a combination of tuberculosis and dropsy. Treatment did not help. Again and again he suffered prolonged nosebleeds. He had already prepared his well-known tomb and he longed to occupy it. But death eluded him.

Hadrian requested his doctor to poison him. Instead, the doctor committed suicide. Next, he asked a slave to stab him, but the slave ran away. He then decided to kill himself and demanded either poison or a sword. His frightened servants refused to comply. He then located a dagger on his own and was about to stab himself when it was snatched away.

Desperate to die, Hadrian moved to Baiae and deliberately ate foods he believed to be injurious to his health. Eventually, his longed-for death came on July 10, 138. His body was cremated and his ashes were deposited in his tomb.

After Hadrian's death, a number of senators who had been awaiting execution were released. His successor Antoninus pled with the Senate to confer divine honors on him. At first this request was refused, but when the elected emperor refused to take the throne until the honors were voted, the Senate reluctantly agreed. Thus, it was voted that Hadrian was a god.

Like Hadrian, Antoninus was famous for building a wall in Britain. His wall, together with the one erected by Hadrian, made Britain safe for Rome for the next two centuries. But the decay which would eventually topple the Empire had already started its deadly work. The good news of Jesus Christ, however, has continued to spread. Moreover, its power and virility have remained.

The story of these tyrants of early Christian times is a bloody tale of incest, perversion, adultery, murder, greed, war, countless executions—and abject misery. In stark contrast, the story of the Christians whom they persecuted is a story of joy, success, transformation. All of this reminds one of a favorite hymn written by Sabine Baring-Gould. The third verse goes like this:

Crowns and thrones may perish, Kingdoms
   rise and wane,
But the church of Jesus Constant will remain;
Gates of hell can never 'Gainst that church prevail:
We have Christ's own promise, And that cannot fail.

Chapter 14

Roads and Communications

Having learned about the lives and reigns of the Caesars and the Herods and the other rulers under whom Christ and the early Christians lived, we turn our attention to the story of a dozen cities in which so many Bible-related events took place. But first, in order to understand these intriguing cities of the New Testament era, we must look into how they received their supplies and how they communicated with one another.

Accustomed as we are to superhighways, air and space travel, we are apt to assume that communications during the lives of the apostles were perhaps even more primitive than they were in colonial America. This is a mistake. Paul and other New Testament workers had easy access to an amazing network of all-weather roads that were unexcelled until half a century ago.

When King William IV appointed Sir Robert Peel prime minister of Great Britain in 1834, Peel was enjoying the sunshine of Rome. Upon receiving the word, Peel—founder of the London police—spared no expense to get to London as soon as possible. The journey took 30 days—a day longer than was required by Caesar's postal system in 54 B.C.

At the death of Augustus Caesar (A.D. 14), the Roman Empire contained 3,340,000 square miles. This means it was slightly larger than the continental United States. And living within this area was a population, estimated by Gibbon, of 120,000,000. To maintain the *Pax Romana*—Roman Peace— it was necessary to be able to move troops and supplies quickly. Thus, good highways throughout the Empire were a number one priority.

In Italy alone there were 372 main routes and 12,000 miles of paved highways. And altogether, throughout the Empire, there were 51,000 miles of paved roads in addition to a large network of secondary thoroughfares. One of these paved roads stretched from Jerusalem to Boulogne!

With such a maze of roads, maps were necessary. These "itineraries" indicated the routes, the distances, and even some of the views along the way. There were even travel books. Will Durant in his *Caesar and Christ*, declared flatly, "Despite all difficulties, there was probably more traveling in Nero's day than at any time before our birth."

Unlike even our best superhighways, Roman roads were built to last centuries. The various Latin names for the ingredients they used have worked their way into English. The bottom layer of a road was made from a four-to-six-inch layer of tightly packed sand known as *pavimentum*. On top of this were placed four layers of other materials.

The first of these was the *statumen*—a foot-thick flow of small stones mixed with clay or cement. This was covered with ten inches of rammed concrete known as the *rudens*. Then over this was spread the *nucleus* made up of rolled concrete from 12 to 18 inches thick. This was then topped with the *summa crusta* made of slabs of lava or silex from eight inches to a foot thick so skillfully joined that the separations were scarcely visible.

Usually the center of the road was higher than the edges, thus providing drainage. A normal highway was 16 to 24 feet wide. For chariots, pack animals, and pedestrians it was fully adequate. As the roads neared a city, part of this width was absorbed by *margines*—sidewalks.

Roman roads were generally straight. This means that they had to cross rivers, marshes, mountains. Frequently their engineers made tunnels, even through mountains of rock. When a road sided a mountain, it was buttressed from beneath with burned brick, stone, and mortar.

Their bridges were excellent and were made to last. From the Egyptians they had learned some of the secrets of hydraulic engineering. When a pier was to be made, they drove double cylinders down through the water and deep into the soil. Both cylinders were made watertight, and the water was pumped out from between them. The space between the cylinders was then filled with cement. Using this method, eight magnificent bridges were built across the Tiber. Some of these are still in use!

Along the highways, a marker was laid down every mile to indicate the distance to the next town. Every ten miles there was a *statio* where one could hire fresh horses. In addition, a *mansio* was erected at every 30-mile interval. At these inns, one could buy supplies and even spend the night. Luke was referring to such a place when he wrote: "When the brethren heard of us, they came to meet us as far as Appii forum, and The three taverns: whom when Paul saw, he thanked God, and took courage" (Acts 28:15).

Mansios had a reputation for immorality, high prices, and even robbery. Wise travelers continued on to the *civities*—cities—where they could secure rooms in safer and more moderately priced hotels.

These highways cost about $10,000 per mile to build. But considering their durability, this was a bargain price. In New Testament times, the entire tax income from the Empire was about $150,000,000. These estimates were made by Will Durant who was thinking in terms of 1940 dollars. In our time this is less than the tax income of many a moderate-sized

American city. But the Caesars did not flinch at spending money on roads.

Realizing that the Romans did not have explosives or heavy modern equipment, people today question how the roads were built. The answer is that they had pulleys, cranes, vertical beams, windlasses, huge treadmills operated by men and animals, and slaves—millions of slaves. Moreover, the Romans were excellent mathematicians.

Normally a chariot could average 40 or 50 miles a day on these roads. But in an emergency they could move faster. At the time of Nero's suicide, a messenger got the news to Galba in Spain, 332 miles away, in 36 hours. Undoubtedly the record, however, was set by Tiberius. He traveled 600 miles in three days to get to the bedside of his dying brother. To manage this, he used relays of chariots.

For those who could afford it, there was an even more pleasant way to travel. This was by the use of the *carruca*—or better yet, the *carruca dormitoria*. This was an ancient sedan chair which was carried by a quartet of men, each with the end of a supporting pole on his shoulder. The carruca dormitoria was complete with beds and for a price one could go to sleep and wake up in another town 50 miles away. Cicero relates that he once met a man equipped with "two chariots, a carriage, a litter, horses, numerous slaves, and besides a monkey on a little car, and a number of wild asses."

Traveling throughout the Roman Empire had several advantages over crossing the same area today. No passports were needed. Roman money could be used anywhere. Likewise, they had some modern conveniences. Letters of credit were available and so were traveler's checks.

A one percent sales tax was levied on tourists and traders. There were no highway patrolmen and no one was arrested for speeding or crossing a yellow line. But soldiers were frequently stationed along the more dangerous routes because of the danger of highwaymen.

One of the Roman highways is especially famous today

because it was used by Paul. Following their conquest of the Balkan Peninsula, the Romans had need of a highway to stretch out far into the East. And so the famous Egnatian Way was constructed. Reaching from Dyrrhachium on the west coast of Macedonia, it threaded its way across the Balkans, Thessalonica, Amphipolis, Philippi, and on to Byzantium— modern Istanbul.

The route followed by this road was a famous one. It had been used by Xerxes, Darius, and Alexander the Great. Portions of this road are still in existence and a number of the original milestones have been discovered.

The Romans did not have a zip code, nor a mail box on the corner. Their empire flourished and died long before the first postage stamp was issued in 1840. But the Caesars did have systems with which to communicate, and some of them were fairly rapid.

When the grain bins in the capital were nearly empty, semaphore signals from Puteoli—one hundred and fifty miles south of Rome—flashed the vital news that grainladen ships were on their way. This type of signalling was done by relays from one high point to another. The Romans also used carrier pigeons.

Mainly, however, the government depended on the firmly established *cursus publicus*—postal system. This organization was perfected by Augustus Caesar, the emperor who was ruling when Jesus was born. The heart of the system was the use of innumerable relays of horses that were stabled every few miles. The port of Neapolis through which Paul and his companions made entrance into Europe after the Macedonian call is now named Kavalla. Kavalla has roots in the Latin word *caballa* which means mare. The port received this name because it was one of the terminals in the Roman postal system.

Each stable along the way was supposed to keep approximately forty horses. With so many mounts available, a letter could be moved 100 miles a day. In times of emergency, of course, this speed could be exceeded. The carrier—often a slave—was known as the *tabellarius*. For a badge, he wore a small bronze shield.

Our English word post comes from the Latin *positus* which means placed. It referred to the way horses were placed at certain intervals along the Roman roads.

The Romans had the greatest and most successful postal system of antiquity. But they were not the originators. The motto on the New York City Post Office: "Neither snow nor rain nor heat nor gloom of night stay these couriers from the swift completion of their rounds" was written by Herodotus. This Greek historian—484-425 B.C.—was referring to a system originated by the Persians!

The Persian king Cyrus—600-529 B.C.—is said to have invented the relay system. It was he who tested the endurance of a horse and determined how far apart they should be spaced.

In the book of Esther—dated by conservative scholars from 485 to 465 B.C.—we read: "And he [Mordecai] wrote in the king Ahasuerus' name, and sealed it with the king's ring, and sent letters by posts on horseback, and riders on mules, camels, and young dromedaries" (Esther 8:10). But long before the appearance of Cyrus, we have the record in Job which says: "Now my days are swifter than a post" (Job 9:25).

But as swift as the Roman post was, it was used almost exclusively for the government. Only on rare occasions could private citizens send mail by the *cursus publicus*, and when this privilege was permitted they had to have an official *diploma*—double-fold—with the the right seals and signatures. The normal private citizen sent his mail by a slave, a tourist, or a special friend.

The apostles, of course, used the Roman roads for much of their travel and correspondence. But they also made use of the sea-lanes. Although Roman ships were driven by sails, some were quite large and could average about six knots per hour. If this seems slow, remember that the Mayflower only averaged two miles per hour!

Many of the ships could carry as many as 600 passengers along with several thousand tons of freight. Passage was cheap. The fare from Athens to Alexandria was less than two American dollars. However, this was for deck passengers, and they were required to provide their own food.

The distance covered by ships in those days is amazing. All of the Mediterranean ports could be reached. In addition, ships went regularly to other parts of the world. In A.D. 80 a book appeared to guide captains to the east coast of Africa and to India. Thirty years before the appearance of this book, Hippalus had charted the frequency and direction of the monsoon winds. And through this discovery, he was able to sail directly from Aden across the ocean to India in about forty days. These charts made him as famous in his day as Columbus is in ours.

But as efficient as the Roman ships were, they were not always available—nor reliable. The compass had not been discovered. There were many wrecks and many pirates. To combat the pirates, Augustus stationed two war fleets near the coasts of Italy. One was at Ravenna on the Adriatic and the other on the opposite side of the Italian boot at Naples. Still, piracy was always a threat. Julius Caesar was especially aware of this, for he was once captured by pirates and held for ransom.

The main threat to shipping, however, was the weather. Few captains were willing to sail between November and March. This was because the cold winters made sailing dangerous. It was because of this hazard that Paul wrote to Timothy: "Do thy diligence to come shortly unto me. . . . Only Luke is with me. Take Mark, and bring him with thee: for he is profitable to me for the ministry. . . . *Do thy diligence to come before winter*" (II Timothy 4:9,11,21).

Another peril to Roman shipping was the periodic typhoons. And any reader of the travels of Paul knows how dangerous these winds could be.

Altogether Paul was shipwrecked four times. (In II Corinthians 11:25, Paul remarked that he had been shipwrecked three times; and so his shipwreck near Malta on his way to a Roman prison was his fourth.) But in spite of all the obstacles to effective communications, transportation and the dessemination of information throughout the Empire was amazingly reliable. By the time of Diocletian toward the end of the third century, the postal system was opened to the entire public. Indeed, the mails became so heavy, Diocletian frequently punished Christians by forcing them to carry mail!

Chapter 15

Rome

The Rome in which Paul was imprisoned was not only the ruling hub of the entire Mediterranean world, it was also the busiest and by far the most interesting city on earth.

Overflowing with luxury, history, and magnificent buildings, it was called the Eternal City. Likewise, knowing of the vice and corruption that lingered along its avenues, and between its more than three hundred public fountains, some—and with good reason—dubbed it The Sewer of the Empire. The Rome in which Paul was chained contained both extremes. But before we start peering and sniffing down its streets, let's see how the great apostle got there. For after all, the letters that Paul wrote and his execution, allegedly just south of the city, are the most far-reaching contributions to the fame of this metropolis on the Tiber.

Having appealed to Caesar, Paul was fettered to other prisoners and sent to Rome for trial. Surviving a terrible shipwreck, he finally landed at Puteoli. There, by permission of Julius, the Roman officer in charge of the prisoners, Paul remained with friends for a week. Then he proceeded to Rome on foot.

At the market of Appius, forty-three miles south of the capital on the Appian Way, he was met by a delegation of Christians who had made the two-day journey in order to greet him and make him feel welcome in the midst of anxiety. Ten miles further up at an inn called Three Taverns, he was greeted by yet another delegation. Here, as Luke recorded, "he thanked God, and took courage" (Acts 28:15).

It is unknown who organized these welcoming parties, but it has been surmised that it was Epaphroditus—the one who had been sent to Paul with a gift from the church at Philippi. Also, one questions why these Roman Christians were so enthusiastic about Paul. A logical reason is that they had been exposed to the book of Romans which Paul had written in Corinth in A.D. 55 or 56—five or six years before his arrival in Italy.

Paul, along with the other prisoners, entered Rome through the Porta Capena. Today this place cannot be precisely identified. But we do know that it was the very beginning of the Appian Way. At the time, a 350-year-old aqueduct—Aqua Appia—passed overhead.

The Appian Way was named after Appius Claudius, the man who started it in 312 B.C. In his later years he was dubbed Appius Claudius Caecus "the Blind." Legend has it that he was so proud of his accomplishment the gods struck him blind. This magnificent highway was used without interruption for over one thousand years.

It has been surmised that Paul's guard Julius was a member of the Praetorian Guard. If this was the case, Paul was probably taken immediately to the Praetorian headquarters on the *Palatine Hill* in almost the heart of Rome. There are some who claim, however, that Julius was a special messenger and a member of the Peregrini. If this is so, Paul would have been led to the Peregrini camp on the *Caelian Hill* to the right.

The rank or order of Julius is unimportant. But to get a general idea of ancient or modern Rome it is necessary to understand that it was compressed onto seven low, flat-topped hills bordered on the west by the gently curving

Tiber.

The Romans then, as now, thought in terms of these hills.

At the time of Paul's imprisonment, Rome was considered to be over 800 years old. Those who accepted the idea that the city was founded by Romulus and Remus—the twins who were nursed by a wolf—believed that it dated back to 753 B.C.

The city Paul faced was a crowded one. Beloch estimated the population to be 800,000, while Gibbon estimated it to be 1,200,000. Half of these were slaves. The total area was less than ten square miles. Having been delivered by Julius "to the captain of the guard," Paul was given the privilege of remaining with a soldier "in his own hired house." Perhaps this special favor was arranged by Julius who had learned to appreciate and trust Paul during their perilous journey.

Rentals in Rome, even in the poorest section, were expensive. Born in Rome in 60 or 61—the approximate time of Paul's arrival—Juvenal knew the city extremely well. To a friend he wrote: "If you can tear yourself away from the games of the Circus, you can buy an excellent house at Sora . . . for what you now pay in Rome to rent a dark garret for one year."

Remembering that Paul once reminded the Corinthians "We both hunger, and thirst, and are naked, and are buffeted, and have no certain dwelling place" (I Corinthians 4:11), we wonder how he could afford even the shabbiest rental—especially with legal fees to pay. The answer is, that the gift brought by Epaphroditus was probably a generous one. It is not difficult to imagine that before he started out on his 850-mile trip to Rome, he said to the Philippians, "Now let's be liberal. Prices here are high, but they are much higher in Rome."

Since Rome had only a tiny middle class, the Romans were unusually rich or desperately poor. The rich built elaborate houses equipped with fine swimming pools and special gardens. Few were higher than two stories. Cellars were practically unknown. Some houses had central heating, but in most the heat was distributed by portable charcoal braziers.

Floors were of concrete or tile. Many had mosaics worked into them. The plumbing was of lead—long sheets were hammered around a slender piece of steel to form a pipe. Expensive statues occupied honored positions and lovely paintings decorated the walls. In addition, most houses boasted of at least one fountain and rain water was drained from the roof by lead gutters.

The rich lived in luxury.

Even though Luke tells us that Paul "dwelt two whole years in his own hired house, and received all that came in unto him" (Acts 28:30), it is unlikely that he lived in an expensive place. Most scholars are agreed that Paul's room or suite of rooms was undoubtedly in one of Rome's large tenement buildings. These block-sized structures were so enormous they were called *insulae*—islands. Since the working classes lived in these apartment houses, and since there was no public transportation, most of the *insulae* were toward the center of the city. This was so the workers could be near their places of employment.

Augustus had decreed that a front of a building could never be more than seventy feet high. But apparently the builders found a loophole in the law and made the back parts higher then the front. Living in Rome in 64, Martial wrote about "a poor devil whose attic is 200 steps up." Shops and offices occupied the ground floor just as they do in modern hotels.

Without street lighting, the areas around an *insula* could be dangerous. Juvenal commented: "And now regard the different and diverse perils of the night. See what a height it is to that towering roof from which a potsherd comes crack on my head every time that a broken or leaky vessel is pitched out a window! See with what a smash it strikes and dints the pavement! There's death in every open window as you pass along at night; you may well be deemed a fool, improvident of sudden accident, if you go out to dinner without having made your will. You can but hope, and put up a piteous prayer in your heart, that they may be content to pour down on your head the contents of their slop-pails."

Unless Epaphroditus had been fortunate in meeting a friend of Paul's when he entered the city, he would have had a most difficult time in finding him. This is because the Romans did not number their houses, and secondary streets did not have names! An ancient comedy of Roman times has survived. The play shows how difficult it was to find an address in Rome. The following exchange is between the slave Syrus and the elderly Demea:

Syrus. Well, I can't recall the name of the man he's gone to see, but I know where he lives.

Demea. Well, tell me the place.

Syrus. Down this way. You know the porch beside the butcher's?

Demea. Yes, of course.

Syrus. Pass this way straight up the street, and when you have gone so far, there's a slope in front of you; go down, and after that there lies a little chapel with an alley close by.

Demea. Where do you mean?

Syrus. Where the big wild fig-tree grows.

Demea. I know.

Syrus. Yes, of course. Heavens! What a fool I am! You must come back again to the porch. Yes, that's also far quicker and less roundabout. Do you know where the wealthy Cratinus lives?

Demea. I do.

Syrus. Well, pass his house, then go left straight down this street, and turn right at Diana's shrine. Before you reach the city gate, just near the pool, there's a bakery with a carpenter's shop opposite. He's there.

Quoted in *Rome: Its People Life and Customs* by Ugo Paoli.

But even if one knew exactly where to go in Rome, he might still face hazards on the way. Juvenal tells us what it was like. "Most sick people here in Rome perish for want of sleep, the illness itself having been produced by food lying undigested on a fevered stomach. For what sleep is possible in a lodging? Who but the wealthy ever get sleep in Rome? There lies the root of the disorder. The crossing of wagons in the narrow winding streets, the slanging of drovers when brought to a stand, would make sleep impossible for a Drusus [a Roman general famous for his strength]—or a sea-calf. When the rich man has a call of social duty, the mob makes way for him as he is borne swiftly over their heads in a huge Liburnian car. He writes or sleeps as he goes along, for the closed window of the litter induces slumber. Yet he will arrive before us; hurry as we may, we are blocked by a surging crowd in front, and by a dense mass of people pressing in on us from behind: one man digs an elbow into me, another a sedan-pole; one bangs a beam, another a wine-cask against my head. My legs are be-splattered with mud; huge feet trample on me from every side, and a soldier plants his hobnails firmly on my toe."

Most Romans who went out at night had a slave precede them with a lantern.

Yes, Rome had a vast sewage system and some of it is still in use. But it was not as efficient as one might suppose. In the days of Paul, one of the main arteries of this network was the *Cloaca Maxima*. Unfortunately this huge drain which was started hundreds of years before Christ, carried rainwater as well as sewage. Even worse, it emptied into the Tiber!

Because these mammoth drains carried storm water, long widemouthed openings had to be made into the streets. The result was that Rome was frequently heavy with the stench of sewage.

An early discovery that had revolutionized Rome was

cement. *Caementicum*, made by mixing volcanic ash with bits of brick, fragments of marble, and sand, was first developed about 200 B.C. This cement was extremely hard and durable.

With it, engineers were equipped to build great buildings, roads, bridges, aqueducts. Altogether, Rome was supplied by fourteen aqueducts. Measuring a total of 1300 miles—the distance from New York City to Omaha, Nebraska—these stone and brick arteries plunged through mountains, across valleys, and over marshes. They delivered three hundred million gallons of water daily.

This seems like an overabundance of water. But the Romans needed it for their elaborate fountains, artificial lakes, vast public baths, and gardens. Moreover, almost every house had a bathtub, and the Romans bathed every day. But then, as now, there were those who connected secretly onto the water in order to avoid payment. This meant that a corps of inspectors had to be employed.

If Epaphroditus arrived in Rome in November, he would not have seen the effects of the almost annual floods. But if his arrival was in the spring, and if he came by sea, he would have shuddered at the devastation brought by the overflowing Tiber. Tacitus wrote: "Men were swept away by the waves or sucked under by the eddies; beasts of burden, baggage, lifeless bodies floated about and blocked their way."

The one-thousand-foot-long Emporium stood on the eastern side of the Tiber. Here, Epaphroditus could see—and smell—the vastness of the trade that flowed in and out of Rome. Crammed with little shops and eager merchants, one could hear chatter and haggling in a dozen languages. In some ways the Emporium resembled the Grand Bazaar in modern Istanbul.

Almost anything could be purchased in Rome. Geese were driven down the highways from far-off Belgium. This was to satisfy the keen demand for goose liver. From other parts of the world came silks, wine, gold, wheat, ivory. Without much searching, one could purchase honey, parchments, drugs, fruit, glass, perfumes, jewelry.

Usually slaves were sold at public auction; and since there was a constant demand, there were many auctions where they could be purchased. At a typical auction, the fettered slave mounted a platform and faced his bidders. A scroll which included a six-month guarantee was draped from the victim's neck. In this document, the name, nationality, skills, and character were listed. Also the person's health was carefully described. No one wanted to pay good money for an epileptic. Usually a doctor was on hand. This man would ask the slave to strip and then he would announce to potential buyers the slave's physical condition.

The price of slaves varied. Dealers often followed the Roman armies. After a victory, a spear was driven into the ground and a buyer began to make purchases. The generals liked this system. It saved them from the problem of dealing with prisoners of war.

As captives were brought to this place to be sold, a wreath was placed around each one's head which stated: *sub corona venire*—to be sold under the crown. The price on the battlefield was as low as $1. This was because it was understood that many of the slaves would die before they reached the markets of Rome. Unused to slavery, many prisoners of war committed suicide. An educated slave might bring a high price. This is because they could be used in the professions. But the price of a laborer was usually less than $100. Horace— 65-68 B.C.—mentioned a slave who was purchased by Marcus Scaurus for $28,000.

At the auction, slaves without a guarantee wore caps and imported slaves had their feet whitened with chalk. One reason for this is that there was a special duty on imported slaves.

Shopping in Rome was like shopping in a modern city. At the time paper money was not in circulation. But there was a sales tax, and it had to be paid in cash.

If Epaphroditus happened to have stopped at a book stall, he would have seen descriptions and lists of titles pasted on the outside walls. Roman book stores were filled with scrolls made of both parchment and papyrus. Also, they contained many codices—bound books. Books were published in editions of one thousand, and considering that they had to be copied by hand, the price was reasonable. Small volumes sold for about $1.50, while deluxe editions which often included the portrait of the author, brought around $3.

Libraries both private and public, were popular. One of the better known of these, *Bibliotheca Ulpia*, was started by Trajan. Quite often there were reading rooms at the public baths. And, as in modern times, the better libraries often displayed the busts of notable citizens.

The Romans loved to eat—and drink. In just the city of Rome 25,000,000 gallons of wine were consumed annually. This works out to about two quarts per week for every man, woman, or child, slave or citizen.

The very rich spent much of their time eating. A typical banquet started at four in the afternoon and continued until late at night. The favorite meat was pork, and according to Pliny a pig could be served in at least fifty forms. A favorite dish—invented by Tiberius—was made from the liver of a pig fattened on figs. At such banquets the tables were decorated with flowers, the air was scented with perfume, and the servants were in crisp livery. Music was also provided, and beautiful women, often in the nude, or nearly so, were displayed.

Exotic foods of every imaginable type were served. Eels and snails were popular, and so were flamingo tongues, ostrich wings, and songbirds.

After a Roman had stuffed himself until he couldn't swallow another bite, he simply excused himself, and went to the *vomitorium*. Seneca complained at this practice. Said he, "*Vomunt ut edant, edant ut vomant*—they vomit to eat and eat to vomit." Having lost their food, they staggered back to the table to eat more.

All sorts of nationalities jostled one another in the streets.

And one did not have to be an expert to sort them out. Most of the Romans were clean-shaven, that is until the time of Hadrian. The down from a youth's first shave was generally dedicated to a god. The backward Britons were conspicuous because of their tattoos and uncouth ways.

Slaves were also easily discernible. Normally a slave wore a tunic and wooden shoes. Also, if he had tried to escape, the letter F, for *fugitivus*, was branded on his forehead. Others had metal collars riveted around their necks. Some of these collars have been preserved. One carries the inscription: *Fugi. Tene me. Cum Revocaveris me d.m. Zonino, accipis solidum*—"I have run away. Catch me. If you take me back to my master Zoninus you'll be rewarded."

The Jewish population was generally about 20,000, and they dressed much as they did in Jerusalem—full beards and all. Although frequently exiled from Rome, most of them usually returned when the emperor's wrath had cooled. On the whole, however, the Jews were not the business leaders of the time. The leading tradesmen were Syrians and Greeks.

The toga was worn only on formal occasions, and it was worn only by Roman citizens. The most distinguished foreigners were not allowed to wear it; and should a citizen be exiled, he was required to leave his toga in Italy.

For normal street wear, the Romans donned blouses. There were no buttons or stockings. Generally the men clipped their hair short. But there were some dandies who sported wigs, and an occasional baldy painted hair on his pate. Fashionable women used rouge, had numerous slaves spend several hours trimming their nails, curling their hair, and darkening their brows and lashes. Some bathed in donkey milk. Indeed, Poppaea—Nero's wife—was so obsessed with this idea, she had a herd of donkeys driven along wherever she traveled!

Since the Romans, until the time of Hadrian, cremated their dead, there were no Western-type cemeteries. And those Romans who did insist on burial were generally entombed by the side of the highways. This they were allowed to do provided the monument was elaborate enough. Remains of such monuments may still be seen along the Appian Way.

Without cemeteries for their dead, the Jews dug underground passages outside the city and placed the bodies in crypts cut into the walls. The soft volcanic stone known as tufa was easily cut. In time, workers, known as fossores, specialized in doing this work. And thus the famous system of catacombs was born. Following the death of Paul, Christians began to make new catacombs. They used these tunnels for their dead, as hiding places, and sometimes extra large rooms were excavated in order to have large rooms where Christians could worship.

The combined length of the catacombs under modern Rome and its environs is estimated to be six hundred miles!

When strangers without funds died in Rome, their bodies were flung into twelve-foot square holes on the eastern side of Esquiline Hill. These graves also served for the disposal of dead animals. Since the pits were not covered, the stench was almost unbearable. This area was something like a city dump. Waste which could not be disposed through the regular sewer system was carted there. This hill was also the place where criminals were executed. When crucified, the victim was not removed from the cross. Instead, the body was left hanging for the birds, wolves, and other beasts of prey which thronged the area.

In his later days, Augustus boasted, "I found Rome built of sun-dried brick; I leave her clothed in marble." And to a large extent this was true. On his way to Paul's lodging, Epaphroditus undoubtedly saw marble on every side. There were long colonnades with tall marble columns, dazzling white public buildings, and many temples in honor of the gods. Suetonius noted that Augustus "restored ruined or burned temples, beautifying these and others with the most lavish gifts; for instance a single donation to Capitoline Jupiter of 16,000 pounds of gold, besides pearls . . . " (*The Twelve Caesars* by Suetonius). To achieve beauty, he did not spare money.

The Colosseum, however, did not exist in Paul's day. Before the time of that building, the throngs flocked to sports events at the Circus Maximus.

Traffic problems in Rome were not as acute as in our larger cities. Still, they had them, and were forced to take drastic action. Julius Caesar decreed:

> ... no one shall drive a wagon along the streets ... in the suburbs where there is continuous housing after sunrise or before the tenth hour of the day, except whatever will be proper for the transportation ... of material for building temples of the immortal gods, or for public works, or for removing from the city rubbish ... (Quoted in *The Appian Way, A Journey* by Dora Jane Hamblin and Mary Jane Crunsfeld).

Whether or not the traffic moved on the right or the left is unknown. Albert C. Rose, however, has suggested that the side of the road "varied depending on where the driver was sitting in relation to his hitch and his carriage."

The Rome of New Testament times was an old and solid city. If during the time of Paul's incarceration, someone had suggested that the Roman Empire would fall, that person would have been considered insane. And yet it came to pass. In 410, Alaric and his Goths swept into Italy. They even captured Rome and looted it for three terrible days. And half a century later it was captured again and looted—this time by the Vandals.

Ironically, the final emperor of Rome was a lad named Romulus—the identical name of the mythical founder of the city!

This terrible drama inspired a Persian poet to write:

"The spider weaves the curtains in the palaces of the Caesars; the owl calls the watches of Afrasiab's towers."

Chapter 16

Athens

Paul frequently retreated. But his retreats were always advances. Hounded by a mob in one city, he simply moved to the next. One priority flamed through his life. This priority was to preach Jesus Christ—everywhere!

Because of the mobs, Paul finally headed toward Athens, the sparkling center of Greek culture. One can only imagine his surging feelings as he entered this city of white marble. Crowned by the Parthenon, already nearly five hundred years old, Athens was a symbol of progressive thought and a democratic spirit.

Coins with the image of Athena—the patron goddess of Athens—stamped on them had been a collector's item in Paul's boyhood city of Tarsus, ever since the conquests of Alexander the Great, Greek power and ideas had been felt throughout the land of the Jews—and beyond.

Undoubtedly while Paul was studying in the various places of learning, books written by and about the various great men of Athens had come to his attention. One can visualize him as a schoolboy winding and unwinding the scrolls of Socrates, Plato, Aristotle, Euripides. Like most educated Jews, Paul spoke fluent Greek. He also probably smiled at some of the older rabbis—especially in the more obscure places. In the past, some of them so hated the Greek language they were convinced it was just as sinful to speak Greek as it was to eat pork! This was in spite of the fact that the Old Testament had been translated into Greek hundreds of years before. The rabbis believed that Hebrew was the sacred tongue.

Paul, however, was most thankful for Greek, for it had become an international language that was understood in the entire Mediterranean world. Thus, with Greek at his disposal, and the use of the Roman all-weather roads, it was much easier to spread the Good News of Jesus Christ.

Like every scholar of his time, Paul knew something of the history of Athens. Around eleven hundred years before the birth of Jesus, the then tiny city was made up of a few villages scattered like seeds around the Acropolis. This flat-topped marble mountain which eventually served as a fortress, now stood before Paul. From a distance it looked like a heavy weight pinning down papyrus sheets on a desk.

In time the citizens of those first few villages conquered their neighbors. But instead of selling their prisoners of war into slavery as was the custom, these progressive Athenians made them into full citizens. Following the success of this radical experiment, a tiny seed of democracy began to grow.

Now, as Paul approached and viewed the Acropolis, his eyes paused for a long moment on the celebrated Parthenon, which dominated the top of the mountain like a magnificently carved, oblong box. Paul had seen many of the fine buildings erected by Herod the Great, but this was equal if not better than any of them.

The marble building with its eight columns in front and back and with six on each side had been erected in honor of Athene during the golden age of Pericles who had ruled the city for thirty-one years.

The actual building was started by the order of Pericles in

447 B.C. It was an age of building temples and each Greek city tried to outdo the other—even though the expense nearly bankrupted them.

Pericles had had a problem with the Parthenon. This had to do with its location. The priests insisted that it be built over the ruins of the old temple of Athene which the Persians had destroyed. But Pericles was obstinate. He insisted on the site used by Themistocles for his unfinished Hectompedon, so named because he had planned to make it one hundred feet long.

The next obstacle was money. When it came time to vote on whether or not to allocate funds for this project, it seemed certain that Pericles' plans would be defeated by the Assembly. But at the most dramatic moment, according to Plutarch, Pericles stunned them. "Very well," he said, "let the cost of these buildings go not to your account but to mine; *and let the inscription on them stand in my name.*"

This suggestion shook the wise ones to the very tips of their beards and turned the tide in favor of Pericles. And so the money—seven hundred talents, perhaps $10,000,000 in our inflated currency—was promptly voted.

Marble for the temple was chosen from that which was quarried at Mt. Pentelicus. No mortar was used anywhere, and since the marble chosen had a fine, iron grain, it was very attractive. Each of the outside columns was six feet two inches at the base, and nearly thirty-five feet tall. Since the joints in these columns are so perfectly matched, tourists have wondered how it was done. The answer is simple. Each "drum" that formed a section of the column was precisely cut and polished. Then a small hole was drilled into the exact center. Next, a round section of olivewood was driven into this hole. A second drum was then fitted onto this one and rotated until its surface ground into the section beneath. With patience, the joints became almost invisible.

But the precise joints are not the great marvel wrapped in this work. Aiming at mathematical and artistic beauty, the planners arranged for the columns to be slightly larger halfway up, and then to gradually taper toward the top. This was done in order to adjust the straight lines of the temple to the "round eye of a man." Likewise, all straight lines were bent just a tiny bit.

These facts indicate that the sculptors and architects of the time had an uncanny understanding of optics and mathematics.

The main purpose of the Parthenon, however, was not just to be a beautiful building. Rather, its main purpose was to house the thirty-eight-foot high statue of Athena made of ivory and gold.

Other buildings also stood on the Acropolis, and one wonders what went through Paul's mind as he viewed them. Is it possible that he remembered how Peter had said to the Sanhedrin, "This is the stone which was set at nought of you builders, which is become the head of the corner" (Acts 4:11)? Perhaps!

Having a large Jewish population, Athens had a number of synagogues, and Paul, as usual, took advantage of this fact. Entering one of these public buildings, he preached Jesus Christ to the usually tolerant Greeks. He also preached Christ in the markets. It was in one of these that he came face to face with the Stoics and Epicureans.

The Stoics were followers of Zeno who had preached in Athens three centuries before. The basic point of his philosophy was to accept all circumstances of life, even poverty and slavery, with a cheerful shrug. And many Athenians accepted this thinking. Indeed, it was even adopted by the Roman Emperor Marcus Aurelius.

The Epicureans had many of the same beliefs as the Stoics. But they liked to emphasize that happiness comes from mental quiet and the absence of fear of the gods. They denied the resurrection vehemently.

Both groups listened to Paul and promptly dubbed him a babbler "because he preached unto them Jesus, and the resurrection" (Acts 17:18)

But with the toleration of Socrates within their beings, they were willing to give Paul a chance, and so they "brought him unto the Areopagus" for a hearing.

Since the Areopagus—Mars Hill—was near the Parthenon, Paul was obliged to climb the Acropolis. And in his day there was a constant stream of Athenians who climbed the hill to present their prayers and offerings to the gods—especially to Athena in the Parthenon. The way to the top was lined with statues of many of the gods, for the Athenians were quite thorough and did not want to neglect the worship of any of them. A vengeful god could cause trouble!

Soon Paul took his place on a flat, marble boulder. With the Parthenon and other marble buildings that had been built to honor the gods on one side, and the sprawling city below, he was ready.

"Ye men of Athens," he began, "I perceive that in all things ye are too superstitious. For as I passed by, and beheld your devotions, I found an altar with this inscription, TO THE UNKNOWN GOD. Whom therefore ye ignorantly worship, him declare I unto you" (Acts 17:22,23).

With this as a springboard, he preached Christ. But although he knew that he was on"trial" before some of the finest minds of the city, he did not soften his message. Surrounded by idols though he was, and with the marble homes of idols nearby, he was extremely candid: "Forasmuch then as we are the offspring of God, we ought not to think that the Godhead is like unto gold, or silver, or stone, graven by art and man's device" (Acts 17:29).

He then told them about coming judgment and the resurrection of Jesus Christ.

The mention of the resurrection so irritated some in the crowd they began to mock him. But others, interested in this "new" doctrine, said, "We will hear thee again of this matter" (Acts 17:32).

Altars to THE UNKNOWN GOD were in many ancient

cities. H. V. Morton relates a curious story in his work, *In the Steps of St. Paul*. "Everyone knew the story of the plague that visited Athens in the sixth century before Christ; and how, after sacrifices had been made to every known god and the plague continued, the services of . . . Epimenides, were requested. He drove a flock of black and white sheep to the Areopagus and allowed them to stray from there as they liked, waiting until they rested of their own free will: and on these spots were the sheep sacrificed 'to the fitting god.' The plague ceased, and it became the custom, not in Athens alone, to erect altars to unknown deities."

It has been frequently claimed that Paul's sermon in Athens was a failure. But this is not really true, for several people were converted during the hearing, and a new church was planted in a thriving city. However, Paul felt he should leave and so he continued on to Corinth.

In comparison to the rugged features of Paul, the polished marble houses on the Acropolis seemed mighty indeed. But as the years eddied by, the Athenians learned that the truth preached by this man of Tarsus was sharper than the chisels of the sculptors—and more enduring.

Sometime during the fifth century the statue of Athena disappeared from the Parthenon, and no one knows what happened to it. Also, about this time, the seeming impossible took place. The Parthenon was converted by the Athenians into a Christian church! And it remained a church for approximately one thousand years.

Then in 1456 Athens was conquered by the Turks and converted into a Moslem city. At the beginning of their rule, the Moslems attached a minaret to the Parthenon and used it as a mosque. Later, the Turks used this former home of Athena to store gunpowder.

Next, in 1687 the Venetians found themselves at war with the Turks, and during a battle they attacked the Acropolis. Amidst the shooting a cannonball went into the Parthenon and touched off the powder. The explosion shattered the roof, blew out some of the walls and caused general havoc.

Thus the building which had endured twenty-one centuries, and had survived the attacks of the Romans and barbarians, fell to the aim of a single cannoneer. But this wasn't the worst disaster that was to befall this priceless work of art.

With the shattered remains of the Parthenon lying about like so many crushed eggs, the people were ruthless with the treasures on the ground at their feet. The Turks ground many of the marble gods into gravel for their roads, and many a statue was used by a peasant for a post in his goat pen!

Fortunately for lovers of art, Lord Elgin received permission from the Turkish Government in 1816 to gather the fragments of the Acropolis and ship them to the British Museum.

Thus, many of the statues seen by Paul may now be viewed by anyone who cares to enter the room where they are displayed. There are other rooms in the same museum, however, where one may view ancient Bibles. Strangely enough, the words Paul preached to the Athenians are well preserved in those Bibles while the marbled gods whom the Athenians were worshiping at the time, have either perished in the form of gravel, or are lingering as fragments in a museum. Moreover, many of the people who read Paul's words in the manuscripts believe them, but practically no one today believes in the Greek gods.

In addition to this, those who visit Mars Hill are now confronted with the message of Paul which he delivered there. That message has been firmly engraved in metal for all to see.

Chapter 17

Corinth

When Paul visited Corinth in A.D. 50 or 51, he had no way of knowing that God was about to use him to bring about within this modern city the birth of a great and influential congregation. Nor did he know that this city was to witness the birth of Christian literature. From a human point of view, these things seemed utterly impossible.

Indeed, if the great apostle had been dominated by recent experience, he would have crumpled with discouragement, for his mission to Athens, as we have seen, was not an immediate, glittering success. And here in Corinth he would face the same type of sneering Greeks who had mocked him on Mars Hill.

Paul, however, trusted in faith—not in experience! And so, the moment he stepped into *Laus Julia Corinthiensis*—the official Roman name—small and then wider doors began to swing wide for him. As a matter of fact, considering everything, Paul's journey to Corinth was one of the most productive journeys of history.

Fortunately for us, the ruins of Corinth remain and one can still see some of the same sights, and feel some of the same pressures that were seen and felt by Paul. Likewise, one can even see the name of one of his converts printed on a paving stone. This printed name is an indication that many influential people were won to Christ at Corinth through his preaching.

The old city of Corinth—the one known by Paul—is just a little over fifty miles directly west of Athens. Today, an excellent highway connects the two cities.

Along this modern highway, just before your arrival in Corinth, you will cross the Corinth Canal. This four-mile-long waterway cuts like a knife across the narrow isthmus that joins the Peloponnesus to Attica. Thus it shortens by two hundred miles the distance ships must travel from the Adriatic ports to Piraeus—the seaport of Athens.

Nero planned this canal in A.D. 66—a few months before the execution of Paul, if one is to believe the current tradition in modern Rome concerning the date of his death. H. V. Morton has described the incident: "On an appointed day the Emperor (Nero) left Corinth at the head of a brilliant gathering and, reaching the site of the canal, snatched up a lyre and sang an ode in honor of Neptune and Amphitrite. He was then handed a golden spade. To the sound of music, he thrust the spade into the earth and collected the sods in a basket which he slung on his back. He then made a speech to the assembled laborers, among whom were six thousand Jews recently captured by Vespasian in the lakeside villages of Galilee, where the Jewish War had begun. It is strange to think that the work of digging in the Corinth Canal was begun by Jewish prisoners of war whose fathers and grandfathers had no doubt heard our Lord preaching on the Sea of Galilee."

Nero, however, abandoned the project. Perhaps he did this because of a superstition that the sea on one side is higher than the sea on the other side. Two years later he committed suicide.

The present canal was started by the French in 1882 and completed by the Greeks eleven years later. In Paul's day, the Romans used an incredible system to cross the isthmus. They moved the ship from one side to the other on rollers!

As far as the New Testament evidence is concerned, Paul was alone when he approached the city. Timothy and Silvanus had been sent to Macedonia to check on the churches at Philippi and Thessalonica. The Corinth which Paul entered was a fairly new city. It was just over one hundred years old.

The general area occupied by Corinth, however, had been inhabited as far back as 5000 B.C. Located in a strategic area for trade, blessed with a vast supply of spring water, and surrounded by the fertile Corinthian plain, it was an ideal place in which to live.

Another attraction to settlers was the flat-topped, lion-colored Acrocorinth mountain which jutted 1875 feet upward just behind the city. This huge mass of rock provided an excellent tower from which to observe an enemy. It was also a convenient place of refuge. And perhaps this is the source of the city's name. Corinth means lookout or guard.

The first sizable number of Greeks moved there about 1000 B.C. From then on, Corinth grew until it was the largest city in Greece. It did not retain this lead, however, for along about the sixth and fifth century B.C. Athens acquired more foreign trade and Corinth became the number two city. Even so, Corinth remained prosperous until 146 B.C. At this time the Roman consul attacked. He captured and utterly destroyed the city. The men were slaughtered, the women and children were sold into slavery.

Following this catastrophe, the razed and dismantled city remained desolate for nearly one hundred years.

But the indomitable career of Corinth had not ended. In 44 B.C. Julius Caesar had it rebuilt as a Roman colony. Next, he colonized it with freedmen and settlers from Italy. Soon the forces that had made the city great in the beginning began to ferment again, and by the time Paul arrived it is estimated that Corinth, together with its double ports, had a population of 600,000.

The Corinth that Paul witnessed was a new one built on

Roman lines. The Lechaion Road, for example, was forty feet wide. It was paved with slabs of hard "slightly colored limestone from the Acrocorinthian quarries." There were sidewalks on either side and smooth gutters to drain away the water from the eaves of the colonnades. And whenever there was a steep rise in the street, broad, easy-to-ascend steps were installed. This street was for pedestrians only. Thus the marks of wheels that mar the streets of Pompeii are not seen on the Lechaion Road.

The city had a vile reputation for debauchery. At the rear of a colonnade one hundred feet long, there were thirty-three taverns. The city had many nightclubs, and standing on the summit of Acrocorinth was the Temple of Aphrodite. This temple employed one thousand priestesses—that is, temple prostitutes.

The reputation of Corinth throughout the Empire was so vile that to insinuate that a man was a "Corinthian" was to insult him. The term referred to gross immorality and people even used the verb "to Corinthianize" which meant to corrupt.

Without a board to forward financial help, Paul had to earn his own living. But this was easy to do in Corinth—the center of the Greek textile industry. Soon he found himself employed on the staff of Aquila and Priscilla. This couple operated a tent-making establishment. Recently expelled from Rome through an edict of Claudius Caesar against the Jews, they were glad to help another stranger in the big city. Also, it may be that they had become Christians while in Rome.

Soon Paul was preaching in the synagogue. Then Timothy and Silvanus appeared with glowing reports from Macedonia. The recently established churches were doing well. Excited with this good news, Paul preached with an even greater intensity and "testified . . . that Jesus was Christ" (Acts 18:5).

But again the Jews would not tolerate such a statement. And so the synagogue was barred to Paul. However, another door opened almost immediately, and this was the home of

Titus Justus, a Roman convert to Judaism "whose house joined hard to the synagogue" (Acts 18:7).

Success followed at once. "And Crispus, the chief ruler of the synagogue, believed on the Lord with all his house; and many of the Corinthians hearing believed, and were baptized" (Acts 18:8).

These victories in Corinth, however, could not keep Paul's mind from drifting back to Macedonia. Those infant churches were close to his heart. Finally, unable to bear the separation any longer, he dipped his pen and wrote: "Paul, and Silvanus, and Timotheus, unto the church of the Thessalonians" (I Thessalonians 1:1).

Paul, at the time, may not have realized it, but those words were the very first words to be written which would be included in our New Testament. The date of this letter can be set at approximately A.D. 50—and we can be quite dogmatic about the date. Why? Because in Acts 18 we read: "And when Gallio was deputy of Achaia [Corinth was the capital], the Jews made insurrection with one accord against Paul, and brought him to the judgment seat . . . And when Paul was now about to open his mouth, Gallio said unto the Jews, If it were a matter of wrong or wicked lewdness, O ye Jews, reason would that I should bear with you: But if it be a question of words and names, and of your law, look ye to it; for I will be no judge of such matters" (verses 12-15).

The problem now is to pin down the date when Gallio was deputy of Achaia. And fortunately this is possible through an inscription found at Delphi. That inscription narrows Gallio's tenure to this period. Alas, Gallio along with his two brothers, Mela and Seneca, was put to death about A.D. 66 through the orders of Nero. This was in spite of the fact that Seneca had been Nero's tutor. (Gallio was forced to commit suicide, and this he did by opening his veins and then lying in a tub of warm water. This was the popular method of the time.)

First and Second Thessalonians, however, were not the only letters that Paul wrote while he was in Corinth. While on his third missionary journey, Paul returned to Corinth and wrote his longest and most influential work—the book of Romans.

Curiously, when Paul wrote to the Corinthians, he exclaimed, "I thank God that I baptized none of you, but Crispus and Gaius" (I Corinthians 1:14). And then in concluding the book of Romans, he mentions that Gaius was his host. Thus, there is strong evidence that Paul wrote—or rather dictated—the manuscript while boarding with one of the two whom he had baptized.

Romans has some strong passages against immorality, and one can easily imagine that Paul composed them after a morning stroll in which his eyes rested on the Temple of Aphrodite on the summit of Acrocorinth.

In the final chapter of Romans where Paul gives credit to Gaius—16:23—he also said, "Erastus the chamberlain of the city saluteth you . . . "

Today, one of the paving blocks in the ruins of Corinth has written on it the following inscription:

ERASTVS PRO AEDILITATE
S P STRAVIT

Interpreted from Latin, this reads: "Erastus, in return for his aedilship, laid the pavement at his own expense." (Aedilship is Latin for commissioner of the streets and public buildings.)

Was this the Erastus to whom Paul referrred? Many researchers think so. At least archaeologists think that the inscription was in existence during the first century after Christ.

Today there is a new Corinth. It is a little to the east of the old one. But for one reason or another, it is just a modest town of 10,000.

Chapter 18

Philippi

As the inter-island ship rocked along through the blue Aegean Sea, Paul and his companions must have tingled with excitement, for after a series of closed doors the Holy Spirit had definitely directed them to Europe. And as a scholar, Paul knew that Europe needed the gospel. No one could deny that.

The preceding days of uncertainty in Asia were now over, and before them lay the Macedonian port of Neapolis—and then, ten miles inland, the ancient city of Philippi. Named in honor of Philip II of Macedon, the one-eyed father of Alexander the Great, it was a spine-tingling place, for in its streets and swamps world history had been battered and twisted into many a new shape. A city of giants and blood, it was almost equivalent to Gettysburg, Verdun, and Waterloo all rolled into one. In 334 B.C., using Philippi as one of his European bases, Alexander the Great had invaded Asia. Now, in stark contrast, Paul, using Asia as his base, planned to invade Europe with the sword of the Spirit. Moreover, this God-intoxicated man from Tarsus was certain of success.

As the ship continued westward toward the flaming sun

behind Mount Athos, Paul's assurance increased. The three who traveled with him were of the highest type. Silas, whom he insisted on calling Silvanus, had the confidence of the brethren in both Jerusalem and Antioch, and Timothy who had joined the band at Lystra was so useful Paul called him "his beloved son." The fourth member was Luke, who had united with Paul at Troas under the most unique circumstances.

On this, his second missionary journey, Paul had planned to visit such cities as Ephesus, Philadelphia, Sardis, and Miletus. But as he wearied along "they . . . were forbidden of the Holy Ghost to preach the word in Asia" (Acts 16:6). Paul, however, was reluctant to give up and so he decided to go to Bithynia. That long province, warmed by the *Pontus Euxinus*—Black Sea—was a rich and fruitful area. (If the borders of this Roman province were still intact, they would include the Asiatic part of Istanbul.) But again he was prevented. This time, "the Spirit suffered them not. And they passing by Mysia came down to Troas" (Acts 16:7,8).

Why the *Holy Spirit* stopped them at one place and the *Spirit of Jesus* in another place is a mystery for the scholars. Undoubtedly both references are to the Holy Spirit. But perhaps on the second occasion the feeling of being forbidden was so strong, Paul was reminded of his experience on the Damascus Road when the voice of Jesus said, "Saul, Saul, why persecutest thou me?" (Acts 9:4). That appeal brought about the most radical change in his life. It turned him from a persecutor into a proclaimer. Likewise, the closed door to Bithynia and the call to Europe entailed a radical change.

It was in Troas that the Holy Spirit's directions came to him in the most dramatic form. "And a vision appeared to Paul in the night; There stood a man of Macedonia, and prayed him, saying, Come over into Macedonia, and help us" (Acts 16:9). Moderns remember Troas as the place where Paul received the startling invitation to Macedonia. But in earlier centuries, Troas was associated with nearby Troy made famous by Homer's story about Helen and the Trojans' wooden horse.

Following the vision, Luke suddenly appeared, and in his account of the voyage as recorded in Acts, he began to use the pronoun "we" at this place. This means that he was now traveling with Paul, and that what we read is an eyewitness account. A doctor, a scholar, and a great writer, was Luke, and Paul had so much confidence in him he referred to him as "the beloved physician."

Remembering the trip, Luke wrote: "Therefore loosing from Troas, we came with a straight course to Samothracia, and the next day to Neapolis; And from thence to Philippi, which is the chief city of that part of Macedonia, and a colony" (Acts 16:11,12).

The sails of the ship must have been taut in order to make the trip in two days, for on a reverse voyage—sailing from Philippi to Troas—it took five days! (Acts 20:6).

Enjoying a straight run to Samothrace is interesting, for all ships making this crossing have to face a strong southward current from Cape Helles. Today, the island of Samothrace, where they stopped in mid-voyage, is remembered as the place where the exquisite statue, Winged Victory, was discovered in 1863. It may be that Paul and his friends even saw it, for it had been mounted for public view by Demetrius in 305 B.C.

Always a student, Paul's blood must have churned as he walked down the colonnaded streets of Philippi, viewed the great amphitheater, paused in front of the marble-columned buildings, felt the cool spray of the fountains, and chatted with the proud inhabitants.

Prior to 361 B.C., the city was known as Krenides. Then in 356 B.C. King Philip II of Macedonia sent in a sizable number of colonists. The gold mines in the vicinity were part of the lure. Philip gave the town his own name and made it an outpost against the Thracians.

Nearly two centuries later in 168 B.C. Macedonia was conquered by the Romans and divided into four sections with

Philippi as part of the first. And then Brutus and Cassius—assassins of Julius Caesar—clashed with the armies of Octavian and Antony just west of the city.

Strolling through Philippi was like viewing a museum dedicated to history! Indeed, one can imagine an oldster tottering up to Paul and saying, "Come! Let me show you where the armies stood. My grandfather fought here. Over there is where—"

The story of this battle where the Roman Republic perished was painfully clear to Paul, for he was from Tarsus. And the citizens of Tarsus had every reason to remember.

Following Caesar's assassination, Cassius—the main instigator of the plot—and his brother-in-law Brutus fled from Rome. Without considering the consequences, the Roman Senate had given them the province of Macedonia and Cyrene. And now the two assassins began to raise armies so that they could defeat Octavian and Antony and become the sole rulers of the Empire.

Armies, however, cost money; and since neither Brutus nor Cassius had any, they devised a system to raise it in a hurry. They forced the cities they controlled to pay their taxes ten years in advance! In addition, they murdered the wealthy and seized their estates. Cassius moved to Tarsus, quartered his soldiers in the homes, and coldly announced that he wouldn't leave until he was paid $9,000,000.

To raise this amount—in those days a fantastic sum—public lands were auctioned, silver and gold vessels from the temples were melted, and the free were sold into slavery. First to be enslaved were boys, then girls, then men and women, and finally old people. Many killed themselves rather than submit. Born between A.D. 10 and 15, Paul must have heard many a spine-tingling tale from those who had been affected by such outrage.

Judea, too, felt this injustice. There, Cassius demanded $4,200,000 and sold the entire population of four towns into slavery.

Brutus, likewise, was ruthless. "When the citizens of Lycian Xanthus refused his demands, he besieged them until, starving but obdurate, they committed suicide en masse" (Will Durant in *Caesar and Christ*).

In September, 42 B.C. the rival armies flooded into Philippi. The camp of Brutus—forming the right wing—was on high ground in front of the city and extended to the mountain across the Egnatian Way. Followers of Cassius manned the left wing—also on high ground. Their fortifications extended into the damp marshes and across that part of the Egnatian Way that connects Philippi to the Symbolon ridge. Cassius also had a lookout on a hill just northeast of Philippi.

Antony and his army reached Philippi by following the Egnatian Way from the west. They camped on the lower, marshy ground in front of Cassius and Brutus. Octavian, who had been ill, arrived in a litter. Together, he and Antony had nineteen legions plus auxiliaries.

Militarily, Octavian and Antony were at a disadvantage. Not only were Brutus and Cassius on higher ground, but they could also get supplies from Asia by way of the sea. In contrast, their rivals could only get supplies from Macedonia—and there was not much available.

With their spears and shields glistening in the sun, the armies glowered at each other for an entire month without making a move. Ghosts bothered Brutus. And Cassius was wary because of the vultures which circled the camp. Cassius knew that Octavian was short of supplies, and because of this, he felt it best to wait and starve him out.

But Brutus was nervous and begged to attack. Cassius pointed to a swarm of bees on one of his standards. This, he declared, was a terrible omen. Brutus, nevertheless, was determined and so the battle started. The army of Brutus, like a racehorse, was too anxious. The men charged before the signal. Then a group slipped around Octavian's flank, killed the guards, and jabbed their spears through his litter again and again until they felt assured that he was dead.

In spite of this strong beginning, however, Cassius and Brutus were defeated, and Octavian, warned through the dream of a friend, had been away when his litter was attacked. Cornered, Cassius commanded his freedman to kill him. Brutus also committed suicide.

At dawn, when Antony viewed the corpse of Brutus, he unbuckled his scarlet general's coat and spread it over the body. Years before, he and Brutus had been friends. But Octavian was not so thoughtful. He hacked off his enemy's head and sent it to Rome to be placed at the foot of Julius Caesar's statue.

Eleven years later, Octavian and Antony—Cleopatra's new lover—went to war against each other. And then during the battle of Actium, off the west coast of Greece, Octavian utterly defeated the fleets of Antony and Cleopatra. Next, Antony and Cleopatra committed suicide. This left Octavian the undisputed emperor of Rome. Four years later the Senate voted him the title of Augustus, and he remained on the throne from 31 B.C. to 14 A.D.

While seeking God's will in Philippi, Paul must have pondered long over these events. But with his knowledge of Jesus, he refused to be bound by a past that had reddened the streets of the city. His eyes were on the future.

Early questioning had shown that there was no synagogue in the city. This was an indication that the Jewish population was extremely small, for generally when there was a minimum of ten male Jews there was also a synagogue. But Paul soon discovered that there was a place of prayer by the riverside where a number of women gathered to worship each Sabbath.

Unlike the rival generals in the Battle of Philippi who simply stared at each other for an entire month, Paul was not afraid to make the first move. And so when the Sabbath came, the team headed for the river just outside the city gate of Philippi. One can imagine Paul's mounting excitement as he strode forward on his way to teach the first Christian lesson that had ever been taught by an apostle on the European continent.

That he would be speaking to a crowd of ladies which included at least one rich one must have been a disturbing thought, for his memory of a previous situation was not pleasant. While in Antioch of Pisidia he was enjoying unusual success when some "women of standing" nearly ruined everything. Indeed, they drove him from the city.

The possibility that these women would turn on him was great. And if they did so, they could ruin his ministry in Macedonia.

As Paul faced the women on the shallow river—probably the Angites—he did so as a veteran of Christ. Soon there was a silence as the women began to listen to this intense man of Tarsus and his friends. (Remember Luke recorded "we went out of the city by a river side, where prayer was wont to be made; and we sat down, and spake unto the women which resorted thither," Acts 16:13).

Among the listeners was "Lydia, a seller of purple, of the city Thyatira, which worshipped God" (Acts 16:14). The fact that Lydia was a dealer in purple indicates that she was a person of means, for purple was one of the most coveted commodities of the time. The name Canaan (Land of the Purple) was derived from this dye, and Phoenicia comes from a Greek word meaning red-purple. Sir William Ramsay estimated that a pound of wool dyed in purple was worth forty English pounds.

Obtaining the dye was an extremely difficult process, but since the demand was great—it was used in the Tabernacle and in the Temple and by the rich—no trouble was spared to obtain it.

The dye was made from the secretions of the hypobranchial glands of certain mollusks, and the different shades were achieved by using various species of the same family of shellfish.

The nationality of Lydia is unknown. Perhaps she was a convert to Judaism. All we know is that she was a worshiper of God. But as she listened to Paul, she was convinced that he was telling the truth and her "heart the Lord opened, that she attended unto the things which were spoken of Paul." And thus she became the first known person to be converted on European soil.

Having experienced the new birth, Lydia became an enthusiastic believer, and soon she and her entire household were baptized. Bubbling with joy, she confronted the team. "If ye have judged me to be faithful to the Lord," she said, "come into my house, and abide there" (Acts 16:15). And Luke added with his marvelous touch, "and she constrained us."

The first church to be planted in Europe was having a marvelous start. Then trouble swooped down from an unexpected source. While the team was on its way to pray, a demon-possessed girl suddenly appeared in the streets. The girl was being led around by her owners. Such sights in a land that believed in oracles was common.

A typical girl like this would speak in a high-pitched voice to a customer, and then her masters would interpret the message for a small fee. With thousands anxious to know the future, it was a profitable business.

Pointing to the missionaries, the girl began to shout, "These men are the servants of the most high God, which shew unto us the way of salvation" (Acts 16:17).

At first Paul and his friends ignored it, but the girl continued to follow and repeat her announcement. Finally, his patience exhausted, Paul said to the spirit that was troubling her, "I command thee in the name of Jesus Christ to come out of her." And Luke adds, "and he came out the same hour" (Acts 16:18).

Incensed because the girl now refused to tell fortunes, the owners seized Paul and Silas "and drew them into the marketplace unto the rulers." Great writer that he was, Luke does not waste words. In this incident, he points out by omitting the names of the others, that only Paul and Silas were arrested. And this makes us wonder why they didn't seize Timothy and Luke. A suggestion is that Paul and Silas resembled Jews more than the others, and since they were being persecuted by Gentiles, this may be the correct explanation. Timothy had a Greek father and Luke was a Gentile.

Undoubtedly the city was anti-Semitic. After the Battle of Philippi, Octavian had settled the area with veterans of the war and had given the inhabitants unique Roman citizenship privileges. Also, he had changed the name of the city to a flattering new one—*Colonia August Julia Philippensis*! At the time of Paul's visit—sometime between A.D. 49 and 52—Emperor Claudius was on the throne, and he had expelled the Jews from Rome. Since Philippi boasted on being "Little Rome," its leaders were quick to follow the laws of the bigger city.

At the public square, the accusers did not waste time. In caustic racist language they said: "These men, being Jews, do exceedingly trouble our city, And teach customs, which are not lawful for us to receive, neither to observe, being Romans" (Acts 16:20,21). Luke then describes what happened. "And the multitude rose up together against them: and the magistrates rent off their clothes, and commanded to beat them. And when they had laid many stripes upon them, they cast them into prison, charging the jailer to keep them safely; Who, having received such a charge, thrust them into the inner prison, and made their feet fast in the stocks" (Acts 16:22-24).

The worst American prisons are palaces in comparison to some of the prisons in the old Roman Empire. With poor ventilation, scanty sanitary facilities, and the worst kind of food, a prisoner's life was a tortured existence. But Paul and Silas were in an even more miserable situation than usual, for in addition to the pain from their wounds their legs were clamped in the stocks, making sleep impossible. Definitely, it was time to complain. But instead of grieving, they sang!

There were other prisoners in the jail, and one can imagine how they may have grumbled at the joyful sounds of the two preachers. But nothing could silence Paul and Silas. The church had been planted in Europe, and they were being strengthened by the risen Christ! Then "at midnight" there "was a great earthquake, so that the foundations of the prison were shaken: and immediately all the doors were opened, and every one's bands were loosed" (Acts 16:26).

On the human level this seems an incredible story, for how could an earthquake remove stocks from the prisoners' feet? Sir William Ramsay, however, has an adequate explanation. "Anyone that has seen a Turkish prison will not wonder that the doors were thrown open: each door was merely closed by a bar, and the earthquake, as it passed along the ground, forced the door posts apart from each other, so that the bar slipped from its hold, and the door swung open. The prisoners were fastened to the wall or in wooden stocks; and the chains and stocks were detached from the wall, which was so shaken that space gaped between the stones" (*St. Paul the Traveler and the Roman Citizen*).

Immediately they were freed, and Paul and Silas might have fled. At the time of Peter's arrest by the order of Herod, this is exactly what he did. But if Paul and Silas had fled, they probably would not have gotten away, for unlike Peter they were in a Gentile city where their Jewish features made them obvious. Moreover, they were being guided by the Holy Spirit. It was in God's plan for Peter to escape, but it was not in God's plan for Paul to escape!

Awakening from his sleep, the jailer was shocked to see the prison doors flung wide. Assuming his prisoners had escaped, he started to commit suicide. But noticing his action, Paul shouted, "Do thyself no harm: for we are all here." The startled jailer then called for lights, "sprang in, and came trembling, and fell down before Paul and Silas" (Acts 16:28,29).

At this point, critics wonder how Paul could see the jailer without a light, and yet the jailer had to have a light to see Paul. The answer is simple. Paul and Silas had been sitting in darkness. In addition, it is easier to notice violent movement in the semidarkness of starlight than to see the features of a man's face.

The jailer, perhaps a son or grandson of a veteran of the Battle of Philippi, may have had the typical Roman fears of omens. Also, his conscience may have been disturbed for placing these noted prisoners in the stocks. But regardless of the source of his fears, he cried out and said, 'Sirs, what must I do to be saved?' "

Prepared by song and prayer, Paul and Silas had an immediate answer, "Believe on the Lord Jesus Christ, and thou shalt be saved, and thy house." And then, following their advice, Paul and Silas "spake unto him the word of the Lord, and to all that were in his house" (Acts 16:31,32).

Deeply repenting of his sins, the jailer washed their wounds, "and was baptized, he and all his, straightway" (verse 33). Were they baptized in the same place where Lydia was baptized? It is entirely possible, for the river was within walking distance. Luke, however, does not mention the place. But he does tell us that the jailer "brought them into his house, he set meat before them, and rejoiced, believing in God with all his house" (verse 34). As a doctor, Luke was interested in their health!

At daylight the magistrates sent officers with instructions to release the prisoners. But Paul refused to be released! "They have beaten us openly uncondemned, being Romans, and have cast us into prison; and now do they thrust us out privily? nay verily; but let them come themselves and fetch us out" (verse 37).

No, Paul was not trying to be difficult. But he was anxious for the new congregation to have a good name in the city!

Thoroughly frightened, the magistrates came and apologized and begged them to leave the city. Now that they were legally free, the former prisoners returned to Lydia's house, "and when they had seen the brethren, they comforted them, and departed" (verse 40).

And thus, amidst misunderstanding and suffering, Europe's first church was founded. Luke's "we" passages end abruptly at this point, and do not continue again until Acts 20:6 where we read, "And we sailed away from Philippi after the days of unleavened bread, and came unto them to Troas in five days; where we abode seven days."

The obvious conclusion is that Luke was left in Philippi to strengthen the church. This conclusion is firmed by II Corinthians 8:18, where Paul said: "And we have sent with him the brother, whose praise is in the gospel throughout all the churches." According to early tradition, this passage referred to Luke.

Chapter 19

Thessalonica

Urgently requested by the magistrates to leave Philippi at once, Paul and Silas, and perhaps Timothy, headed southwest on the Egnatian Way for Thessalonica. Having been severely beaten in Philippi, Paul and Silas must have been in pain as they trudged along.

The first large city on the way was Amphipolis—about twenty miles from Philippi. Today, this city rates less than one hundred words in a typical Bible dictionary. This is because there is no New Testament record of a church being founded there. However, the city did have a Christian witness in the succeeding years. This we know because remains of a Christian community were unearthed in 1920. Today, the city has disappeared.

But during Paul's time, Amphipolis—on the left bank of the Strymon—enjoyed a certain fame, especially with history buffs. The family of the Greek historian Thucydides—460 to 400 B.C.—owned mining rights there; and following the Roman conquest, it eventually was made the capital of that part of Macedonia.

In addition, Amphipolis had supplied Alexander the Great with three of his star naval officers: Nearchos, Androsthenes, and Laomedon. In 1912 a great stone lion was uncovered here, and it is thought that it was erected in honor of Laomedon.

The Ptolemies of Egypt also originated in this city. Another bit of history that was constantly dripping from the loose tongues of the guides concerned the civil war between Pompey—the one who made Palestine a Roman province in 63 B.C.—and his former father-in-law, Julius Caesar. Following utter defeat at Pharsalus, Pompey boarded a ship at Amphipolis and sailed for Egypt. In Egypt the defeated general was knifed to death as he stepped ashore.

At the end of another day's journey, Paul and his friends reached Apollonia, an additional thirty miles away. From here it was only thirty-eight miles to Thessalonica. How they traveled, no one knows. It can be assumed they walked.

Thessalonica was the type of city Paul liked to cultivate for Christ. It was the largest commercial center in the southeastern section of Europe. Firmly situated on both the Via Egnatia and the Aegean Sea, it was in easy contact with the rest of the world. Paul believed that a strong congregation here could be a spiritual watershed to other areas.

In the beginning, among the tiny villages at this place, was one named Therma. It was probably so named because of the nearby Thermaic Gulf. Then about 315 B.C., Cassander, a general who had served under Alexander the Great, united the villages into a city. He named the new combination in honor of his wife Thessalonica, a stepsister of Alexander the Great.

Around 168 B.C. Thessalonica, at this time a walled fortress, fell to the Romans in the battle of Pydna. This concluded the Roman conquest of Macedonia. Eighteen years later, Thessalonica was made into the capital of the second of the four districts into which the Romans had divided the country. Next, during the war between Caesar and Pompey about a century later, Pompey used Thessalonica as his base. This means that Thessalonica was deeply associated with the loser, and in those days of vengeance this could mean trouble. But the city redeemed itself a short time later when it backed Octavian and Antony in their war against Brutus and Cassius. Octavian was a man to reckon with, for he became the Caesar Augustus of Luke 2; also he was the grandnephew of Julius Caesar. And, as a reward for its help, Octavian made Thessalonica a free city.

At the time of Paul's visit, Thessalonica was a prosperous city with a large Jewish colony. Today, Salonica—the modern name—is proud of Paul's visit, and eager guides are anxious to show tourists the place where he entered the city—and the place where he left. According to a legend, when Paul stepped though the gates he knelt to pray. This *very* spot has been marked by a circular piece of marble.

Luke's record of Paul's visit to Thessalonica recorded in Acts has been the basis for serious debate. The first of the problems has to do with Acts 17:6 and 8. In the original, the officials mentioned in these passages were referred to as *politarchs*—literally, city rulers. This fact was used by critics to support their claim that the book of Acts was unreliable. Part of their claim was because this word is not found elsewhere, or so they thought. Since then, however, at least sixteen examples of the term have been discovered. Indeed, the word was found on a Roman arch in Thessalonica.

Since Thessalonica had been made a free city, the politarchs had the freedom to make their own decisions about internal affairs.

Another problem concerning Paul's visit to Thessalonica has to do with the length of his stay. Since there was a large Jewish population, the city had a synagogue—Paul's favorite place to start a new work. Luke wrote: "And Paul, as his manner was, went in unto them, and three sabbath days reasoned with them out of the scriptures" (Acts 17:2).

Three sabbaths in a row could mean just a little over two weeks—the length of a revival campaign. And yet we have the following facts: (1) A strong church which followed through

149

with a vigorous missionary program was established (I Thessalonians 1:8). (2) Paul got a full-time job at his tent-making trade (I Thessalonians 2:9). (3) While in Thessalonica, Paul received two gifts from the church at Philippi (Philippians 4:16).

That all of these accomplishments and activities could be crammed into such a short period seems amazing. And yet all things are possible with the Lord, especially when we are fully surrendered! Moreover, the world-shattering convulsions of Pentecost took place in even less time.

Sir William Ramsay thought that the "three sabbaths" merely referred to the times that Paul taught in the synagogue. Indeed, he was so certain that Paul was in Thessalonica for a longer period, he suggested that he was probably there from December of A.D. 50 to May of 51. And Sir William may be right,

As usual, however, a riot was stirred up. "But the Jews which believed not," wrote Luke, "moved with envy, took unto them certain lewd fellows of the baser sort, and gathered a company, and set all the city on an uproar, and assaulted the house of Jason, and sought to bring them out to the people.

"And when they found them not, they drew Jason and certain brethren unto the rulers of the city, crying, These that have turned the world upside down are come hither also" (Acts 17:5, 6).

Since Thessalonica was a large city, the fact that it was all in an "uproar" indicates that Paul had made a great impression. And this fact comes to sharp focus when we recognize that the Romans were expert in keeping civil disorders to a minimum.

In the presence of the politarchs, the mob shouted, "These all do contrary to the decrees of Caesar, saying that there is another king, one Jesus" (Acts 17:7).

Insinuating that the Christians had flouted the Emperor, they touched a sensitive spot. True, Thessalonica was a free city. But the accusation of treason carried terrifying implications. Having had a pair of semi-sane emperors on the throne—Tiberius and Caligula—the politarchs were unusually wary. A single word uttered by the Emperor could result in the loss of their freedom or even mass crucifixions. Tacitus declared that Tiberius took in a good share of the Empire's income by making such accusations and then forcing the accused to forfeit either their cash or their lives.

Considering the situation, the politarchs acted with mildness when they released Jason and the others on bond.

That evening the congregation sent Paul and Silas off to Berea—some fifty miles to the west. Paul left with a heavy heart.

Berea was a lovely city in Macedonia. Lying at the foot of Mt. Bermius and on a tributary of the Haliacmon, it was one of those places where most people would like to linger. Once again Paul started to preach Christ in the synagogue. And here he found the Jews more receptive. "These were more noble that those in Thessalonica, in that they received the word with all readiness of mind, and searched the scriptures daily" (Acts 17:11).

But once again a mob appeared. This time the ruffians came from Thessalonica, and they caused so much disturbance that Paul felt it wise to move on.

Having been grossly mistreated by the Jews of Thessalonica, Paul might have forgotten the church he had founded. But he did not. Instead, he wrote them a letter from Corinth, and then followed it with another. These letters are known as First and Second Thessalonians. The first of these letters became the very first writing that was gathered into the collection of books that we now call the New Testament. The letters are concerned with the resurrection, death, judgment, obedience— and especially the second coming of Christ.

Paul longed to see the Thessalonian brethren again. In the first letter, he wrote: "Wherefore we would have come unto you, even I Paul, once and again; but Satan hindered us" (I

Thessalonians 2:18).

How did Satan hinder him? Sir William Ramsay thinks that he was hindered because of the bonds which were extracted from Jason and the others to guarantee that there would be no more disturbances. If Paul had returned there might have been another mob and those bonds would have been forfeited and Jason put into custody.

Chapter 20

Ephesus

The Ephesus that Paul knew was a glittering city of wealth, fame, power, incredible superstition—and flagrant sin. It was also the largest Asian city in the Roman Empire. Ships from every nation crowded its ports.

But whatever its commercial attributes might have been, its greatest hold on fame was attached to its Temple of Artemis— also known as the Temple of Diana. And without doubt when Paul arrived in Ephesus in A.D. 52-55, he saw the temple and the eager crowds milling around it. The massive structure with its rows of marble columns was one of the Seven Wonders of the World, and like the Eiffel Tower, was almost impossible to avoid.

After visiting it, an ancient traveler, according to H. V. Morton's book, *In The Steps of Paul*, wrote: "I have seen the walls and hanging gardens of the old Babylon, the statue of Olympian Jove, the Colossus of Rhodes, the great labor of the lofty pyramids, and the ancient tomb of Mausolus. But when I saw the Temple of Ephesus towering to the clouds, all of these marvels were eclipsed."

This temple, however, along with most of the old city where Paul had walked and labored, disappeared completely from view for many a century, and its existence was so forgotten, crops were cultivated on the soil that covered it. And then J. Turtle Wood, an Englishman, went to Turkey in 1863 to see if he could locate the Temple of Artemis, and the rest of the city.

Attracted by a weed-covered pond, Wood began to sink shafts. But these deep holes revealed nothing of real value. He, however, was an indomitable man, and to find the lost temple became an obsession. Fearlessly he tried again and again. But always without result. And along with discouragement, he had a continuing battle with malaria, thieves, the Turkish government, and a gnawing lack of funds. He was being financed by the British Museum, but its directors were determined not to waste a penny.

As the natives watched him at work, they saw a bearded man dressed in a tightly-buttoned frock coat and crowned with a stovepipe hat. All sorts of ridicule were flung at him by the local population, and a large section of the more illiterate questioned his motives. Perhaps he was out to free evil spirits. Or perhaps all of this digging would unleash another earthquake!

But neither illness, broken bones, nor ridicule could deter J. T. Wood. Finally, after six years of near-fruitless labor, he dug into the theater which is mentioned in Acts 19. There, he uncovered a number of inscriptions which had been written on thin slabs of marble and fastened to the walls.

Among these were copies of letters from post-New Testament emperors—Hadrian (ruled 117-138) and Antoninus (ruled 136-161)—which had been addressed to the Magistrates, Council, and people of Ephesus. The epistle from Antoninus reproached the Ephesians because they did not agree with the plans of Vedius Antoninus who had a plan to improve the city.

These slabs were of historical interest, but they did not give a clue to the location of other important buildings in the city. If only he could find a map!

Then, on clearing the southern entrance to the theater, Wood discovered a long inscription inscribed on several huge blocks of marble which had been carefully dowelled together. This inscription described about thirty silver and gold images, weighing from 3 to 7 pounds each. These images—probably resembling those made by Demetrius—were described by Wood as of "Artemis with two stags, and a variety of emblematical figures."

Undoubtedly this inscription had been placed in this prominent place in order to satisfy the vanity of a certain Roman citizen, C. Vibius Salutarius. This gentleman who had lived in Ephesus some fifty years after Paul's ministry, had presented the Temple of Artemis with these images. In addition, according to the inscription, he had set up an endowment to provide money to keep the images polished!

Ah, but that isn't all that was mentioned. Having provided for the images and their upkeep, the financier insisted on certain procedures. One of these was that on special days, including the birthday of Diana, the images were to be carried in a procession from the Temple to the theater. Moreover, he decreed that the procession was to include "two curators of the temple ... conquerors in the games ... a staff bearer and guards." He also described the route that was to be followed with extreme care. And in his instructions he mentioned the Magnesian gate and the Coressian gate.

Wood's heart fluttered as he read the long inscription. Intuitively, he realized that this wealthy Roman wanted as many people as possible to see his gifts, and thus he had arranged for the bearers to follow a long, circuitous route. And now if he could only find and identify those gates! He redoubled his efforts.

By the last day of 1869 he had not only discovered the gates, but he had also located the site of the Temple. It was a mere twenty feet beneath the top of the ground on a rather modest elevation. At the time, he had been suffering from a three-week attack of malaria. But even though he had chills and his bones ached, he continued to excavate until he had located a number of columns and the celebrated carved drums. These drums distinguished the Temple of Artemis from other temples in the Greek world and thus proved he had located the correct temple. Concerning one, J. T. Wood wrote: "Until this immense block, six feet high, and more than six feet in diameter, was raised to the surface, I had an anxious time of it. For any mischievously disposed person might have chopped all the sculptures off in the course of a single night. It took fifteen men fifteen days to raise it up to the surface, and I put it at once into a temporary wooden case, to protect it from injury."

Today this drum may be seen in the Ephesian section of the British Museum.

The Temple of Artemis has been carefully reconstructed in model form, and from the excavations and passages in ancient literature, its dimensions are quite definitely known. The building was just under 164 feet wide and a little over 342 feet long. Altogether, there were one hundred outside columns. The columns were 6 feet at the base and slightly over 55 feet high. Pliny tells us that 36 of them were sculptured. The roof was of "white marble tile."

The statue of Diana, prominently displayed in the temple, was that of a multibreasted woman, considered a fertility goddess. Also, "the image which fell down from Jupiter" (Acts 19:35)—probably a stony meteorite—was housed there.

Since the Temple was solidly built, it served as a sort of international bank, and it is said that the first type of traveler's checks were issued from here. During the first century, there was an annual month-long festival in honor of Artemis which drew as many as half a million people from all over the Mediterranean world.

Wood's discoveries in Ephesus have all underlined the accuracy of the New Testament—and especially that of the book of Acts.

The history of Ephesus is pitted with almost incredible mystery and legend. It is claimed that the first city was founded three thousand B.C. and that it acquired its name from a fierce Amazon queen. The Amazons, according to legend, were from a race of warrior women who captured and enslaved men. And so determined were they, it is claimed, they burned off their right breasts to enable them to draw back their bowstrings farther and shoot their arrows with better ease. (It has been suggested that the idea of the Amazons came into being because Hittite soldiers on Egyptian monuments are shown wearing robes reaching to the feet.)

Ephesus was their largest city.

By around one thousand B.C. their city had vanished. And then some Athenians decided that they would build a new one. But first they consulted the Delphic Oracle for instructions. There, the mysterious voice told them that a fish would mark the *general* place and that a boar would lead them to the *precise* location.

Soon, a fish jumped out of a fire where it was being roasted. A live coal attached to it set the bushes on fire, and this fire frightened a boar which led the picnickers to the right spot. But legend as this must be, the Ephesians believed it, and as late as A.D. 400 the statue of an honored boar stood just outside the gates!

Extremely well located, Ephesus was an ideal stopping place between East and West. Many important roads met there as did the sea-lanes. And then during the reign of Attalus II—one of the kings of Pergamus—an engineer made a serious mistake. Seeking to make the River Cayster scour better, he narrowed the mouth of the stream on the north side, and built an extensive mole into the sea. But his works had an opposite effect to what he had planned.

The surrounding mountains were saturated with loose, disintegrating stone filled with mica-schist. Normally, this debris was washed away by the sea. Now, the narrowed banks and mole stopped this and the harbor began to silt up until it became unusable. This tended to slow the development of Ephesus. The Romans attempted to remove the silt in A.D. 65, but the task proved so enormous they gave up. In time, Smyrna began to replace Ephesus as a seaport.

Jealous of the prosperous Ephesians, the Lydian Croesus launched an attack in the sixth century B.C. The terrified Ephesians sought protection by tying a series of long ropes from the highest part of the temple to the city three-quarters of a mile away. But Artemis was unable to help them. Croesus then destroyed the city and moved the population further inland toward the temple. Indeed, he repaired the temple and provided a set of column drums with his name inscribed on them. These may be seen in the British Museum.

Following the labors of Croesus, the city and temple continued to expand. Then in 365 B.C., the year Alexander the Great was born, a lunatic by the name of Herostratus, wishing to commemorate his name, set the temple on fire and destroyed it.

Under the spell of Artemis, the Ephesians immediately hired a famous architect—either Deinocrates or Cheirocrates—and began to rebuild on a grand scale. In the midst of construction, Alexander the Great appeared in 334 B.C. Utterly charmed, the youthful conqueror offered to pay the entire cost of reconstruction and to provide funds for perpetual care. However, he had a condition. That condition was that his name be inscribed on the building!

To this request, the Ephesians came up with the world's most diplomatic refusal. It would be wrong, suggested their spokesmen, for one god to make a dedication to another god! Highly pleased with this retort, Alexander directed that the Ephesian tribute money be retained by the city and used for the temple.

Ephesus mushroomed again in size—and pride. About 190 B.C. the Romans defeated Antiochus the Great. They forced him to turn Ephesus over to them, and they in turn gave the city to Eumenes II, king of Pergamos. Next, in 133 B.C., the Romans took the city back and made it the capital of their Asian province. In A.D. 29, Ephesus was severely damaged by an earthquake. Generously, Tiberius hastened to repair the damage—and claim credit on his coins for having done so.

Again and again the temple was damaged. Nevertheless, it was always restored or rebuilt—and generally on a grander scale. Across the centuries, the temple became an asylum where the pursued could find refuge.

For a while, the safety zone was confined to the temple itself. And then Alexander the Great increased the area of refuge by decreeing that anyone who was within a *stade* of the temple was safe. The distance of a stade was determined by Mithridates who shot an arrow from a corner of the roof. This distance of two hundred yards was officially felt to be too long; but being generous, and having a firm faith in Artemis, the rulers did not object.

After Mark Antony occupied Ephesus in 41 B.C. and was joined by Cleopatra, he doubled the radius of the safety zone. This meant that any fugitive who managed to get within four hundred yards of the temple was safe.

The Temple of Artemis, however, did not stop the Ephesians from emperor worship, for Artemis was considered to be merely a god among many gods. As the Roman rule flowered, the emperors insisted that a temple be built for emperor worship. During this time, any city which managed to have such a temple was highly honored and was given the title *Neocorus*—Temple Warden. Thus, the competition to have such a temple was severe.

History tells us that Ephesus won this title during the reign of four emperors. And thus her pride increased.

When Paul entered the city to stay and establish the church in A.D. 53, he had many human reasons to be discouraged. Besides emperor worship, the worship of Artemis, and a strong Jewish element, the city was drenched in immorality— and was exceedingly superstitious. An inscription on a building proclaimed: "If the bird is flying from right to left, and settles out of sight, good luck will come. But if it lifts up its left wing, then, whether it rises or settles out of sight, misfortune will result."

On a previous trip to Ephesus (Acts 18:18-21), Paul had arrived with his old friends, Priscilla and Aquila. This couple had worked with him in Corinth and were strong in the faith. Thus, when Apollos of Alexandria went to Ephesus and began to preach, this couple gave him doctrinal instruction which he gladly accepted.

Again, Paul started his work in the synagogue where he continued to preach for three months, and then he moved into the lecture hall of Tyrannus where he remained for "the space of two years." And so successful was he, Luke reported: " . . . all they which dwelt in Asia heard the word of the Lord Jesus, both Jews and Greeks" (Acts 19:10).

In addition to this, the gospel overcame the superstitions of many. Luke wrote: "Many of them also which used curious arts brought their books together, and burned them before all men: and they counted the price of them, and found it fifty thousand pieces of silver" (Acts 19:19; it has been estimated that this was equivalent to $10,000).

All of this success, however, infuriated the silversmiths, for much of their living came from making silver shrines of Artemis. Demetrius was especially incensed. After gathering the silversmiths, he expounded his complaint: "Sirs, ye know that by this craft we have our wealth. Moreover ye see and hear, that not alone at Ephesus, but almost throughout all Asia, this Paul hath persuaded and turned away much people, saying that they be no gods, which are made with hands" (Acts 19:25,26).

Demetrius then whipped up the crowd until the "whole city was filled with confusion" (verse 29). Next, having caught Gaius and Aristarchus, friends of Paul, they rushed them into the great amphitheater—a stadium-like affair that seated 24,500.

Utter confusion followed. Finally, Alexander was helped to the front and he managed to get the mob's attention. But when it became apparent that he was a Jew, the people became hysterical and for two hours they kept repeating as with one voice "Great is Diana of the Ephesians"(verse 34).

Undoubtedly many would have been killed had it not been for the town clerk who miraculously established quiet and then said: "Ye men of Ephesus, what man is there that knoweth not how that the city of the Ephesians is a worshipper of the great goddess Diana, and of the image which fell down from Jupiter? Seeing then that these things cannot be spoken against, ye ought to be quiet, and to do nothing rashly" (Acts 19:35,36).

He next pointed out that they could take the matter to court. This calmed them and "he dismissed the assembly."

Paul, however, felt that the Holy Spirit was directing him to another city, and so after embracing the disciples he left for Macedonia.

Paul's years in Ephesus had been fruitful in spite of some periods of unpleasantness. In his first letter to the Corinthians, he mentioned having "fought with beasts at Ephesus" (15:32). Does this mean Paul was imprisoned in Ephesus? Perhaps! Indeed, there are scholars who think that some of his prison epistles were written in Ephesus. Writing to the Corinthians, Paul said: "For we would not, brethren, have you ignorant of our trouble which came to us in Asia, that we were pressed out of measure, above strength, insomuch that we despaired even of life" (II Corinthians 1:8).

To many, that passage refers to a deeper trouble than was caused by Demetrius at the theater.

Another argument in favor of an imprisonment in Ephesus centers around the slave, Onesimus. Having fled from his master at Colossae (Colossians 4:9), he went to Paul who was in prison to request help. Paul responded to his plea by writing the beautiful letter known as Philemon.

Since Colossae was only one hundred miles east of

Ephesus, and Rome was at least one thousand miles west of Colossae, it is resonable to assume that it would have been more likely that Onesimus would have called on Paul at Ephesus. And this idea is especially significant when we realize that on a trip to Rome, Onesimus would have had to cross two oceans and hundreds of miles of land. True, passports were not required. Still, many embarrassing questions might have been asked, and in Roman times runaway slaves found it almost impossible to escape.

It must be admitted, however, that most scholars believe that Paul's imprisonment—the one in which he wrote his epistles—was in Rome rather than in Ephesus.

In Acts 20:16,17 we see Paul at Miletus. Here, he had arranged for the Ephesian elders to come over and see him. But why didn't he stop at Ephesus only a short distance away? Luke tells us: "Paul had determined to sail by Ephesus, because he would not spend the time in Asia: for he hasted, if it were possible for him, to be at Jerusalem the day of Pentecost" (Acts 20:16). That was a good reason. And yet he might have arranged to have reached Miletus a day or two earlier, and then spent some time in Ephesus.

But there is a hint that he wanted to avoid Ephesus. Why? J. T. Wood made the interesting suggestion that perhaps an inscription had been posted on the theater forbidding him to preach there. And it is quite possible that that was at least part of the reason. Paul was a law-abiding man!

Chapter 21

Antioch

When it concerns the church, Antioch was a city of firsts. It was the first city to have a Gentile congregation. It was the first city to send out missionaries. It was the first city to provide relief for another congregation, and it was the first city in which followers of Christ were sneered at as "Christians."

In addition, the church at Antioch had some of the most colorful experiences recorded in the New Testament. It was here Paul withstood Peter to the face, and it was here the controversy over circumcision stirred to the surface.

Ah, but what Antioch are we writing about? The New Testament speaks of two Antiochs, and history lets us know that there was another fourteen. Sixteen Antiochs existing at the same time and in the same approximate area sounds like an interesting story. And it is! But our concern here is with the Syrian Antioch, the Antioch of this chapter.

After long bouts of drinking, Alexander the Great died in Babylon on June 28, 323 B.C. He was not yet 33. Since he had not written a will, an officer went to his bed just before his death, and asked to whom the kingdom should go. Alexander is reported to have replied, "To the strongest!" Eventually,

ANTIOCH

Seleucus—one of Alexander's noted generals—became the ruler of Syria. Burning with a passion to perpetuate the name of his father Antiochus, Seleucus founded and named the sixteen cities after him. Since, however, it was an ancient practice to alternate the name of a family—the name going to the grandson rather than the son—it is debated whether Seleucus named the city after his father Antiochus or after his son Antiochus.

The approximate site of Antioch was selected by Alexander the Great. At the end of the battle of Issus in which he defeated the Persian king, Darius III, Alexander marched south to Phoenicia where he began his seven-month siege of Tyre. On the way, he paused just east of the city. Here he drank from a spring. And since the water was so refreshing, he impulsively decided to build a city near the spot. But since he was in the midst of planning a new campaign, he merely stayed long enough to order a temple built for Zeus.

Around 300 B.C., Seleucus made a series of sacrifices to the local gods and pled their guidance in founding the city. As the sacrifices were burning, so insists the incredible legend, an eagle—the bird of Zeus—swooped down and snatched a piece of meat from the flaming altar. Seleucus then hurriedly commanded his son to follow the eagle on horseback. The eagle flew to the temple of Zeus and dropped the meat on its altar. Thus convinced of the location, Seleucus asked his architect, Xenarius, to lay out the city.

According to the procedure of the period, army elephants were stationed at the points where the towers in the wall were to be built, and the streets were marked with wheat. "The size of the settlement did not fill the whole site. Seleucus built on the level ground near the river in order to avoid the wash from Mount Silpius. The settlement lay in an oblong shape, between the river and the road that in Roman times became the colonnaded main street. The agora or marketplace, which is still the industrial and commercial quarter of the modern city, lay along the bank of the river" (*Ancient Antioch* by

Glanville Downey).

The entire city, including the section for Europeans and the one for Syrians, covered less than a square mile. And since New Testament Antioch had a population estimated at around half a million and was second in size only to Rome and Alexandria, this part of the city was a mere nucleus.

Glanville Downey wrote: " . . . the streets had no relation to the river [Orontes], but were very carefully oriented with respect to the sun and the prevailing winds; they were laid out to take advantage of shade in the summer and sun in the winter, and the direction of the main avenues along the long axis was calculated so as to catch the regular breeze which blew from the sea up the valley of the Orontes in the summer."

And thus Syrian Antioch, located on the bank of the Orontes, at the top of the Fertile Crescent, came into being. With Mount Silpius in the background, the navigable river connected the city to the Mediterranean twenty miles to the front, and with a favorable climate, Antioch was ideally located.

A suburb of Antioch, known for its beauty, came to be so closely associated with Antioch, the two cities were frequently named together. With its cypress trees, Temple of Apollo, fountains, and waterfalls, Daphne became a popular resort. Its popularity grew with the centuries. An Olympic stadium was built there and the Olympic Games of Antioch rivaled those of Greece. Roman emperors and Hellenistic kings liked to spend their summers there. The "park" sported a theater, private baths, expensive villas—and "houses of pleasure." Gradually the worship of Apollo was combined with the worship of Artemis, and this added to the vile reputation of the place for being a cesspool of immorality.

In the middle of the first century B.C., the seacoast around Antioch became a hiding place for pirates. During his assignment to clear the Mediterranean of these privateers, Pompey put Antioch and the rest of Syria under Roman control. He made Antioch the capital of the new province and gave it freedom to manage its own internal affairs.

Soon the Romans began to beautify Antioch. They were lavish with colonnades, fountains, public buildings. One of the most famous buildings erected at this time was the basilica of Julius Caesar which he named the Kaisarion—after himself. Part of the ruins of this can still be seen. Roman statues of emperors and gods lined the streets, and an amphitheater was constructed for gladiatorial fights.

When Antioch was jolted by a severe earthquake in A.D. 37, Caligula sent help at once to repair the damage. And having inherited a full treasury from Tiberius, he spent money lavishly. Indeed, he built many new buildings.

While these things were going on, Jesus Christ was crucified outside the gates of Jerusalem some 300 miles to the south. And then following His resurrection, ascension, and the outpouring of the Holy Spirit on the day of Pentecost, the church leaped forward—especially in Jerusalem.

As the church in Jerusalem expanded, deacons were chosen to look after the business affairs of the church. Among the seven chosen was "Nicolas a proselyte of Antioch" (Acts 6:5). All went well until the stoning of Stephen—another of the deacons. Persecutions followed and many of the believers were "scattered abroad."

Some went to Phenice (Phoenicia), others to Cyprus, and still others to Antioch. These refugees continued to preach "but unto the Jews only" (Acts 11:19). Others, however, felt that the words of Jesus should also be preached to non-Jews. Some of these men were from Cyprus and Cyrene "which, when they were come to Antioch, spake unto the Grecians, preaching the Lord Jesus" (Acts 11:20). Was Nicolas, the proselyte of Antioch, one of these? We are not told.

This mission to the Greeks in Antioch was so successful Luke wrote: "And the hand of the Lord was with them: and a great number believed, and turned unto the Lord" (Acts 11:21). Among the members of this congregation was Manaen, an intimate friend, and perhaps even the foster-brother of Herod the Tetrarch (Acts 13:1).

The congregation was spiritually well equipped. "Now there were in the church that was at Antioch certain prophets and teachers" (Acts 13:1). Moreover, the leaders in the congregation were firm believers and dedicated men.

When the story of the success of the church at Antioch reached the brethren in Jerusalem, they were delighted. Indeed, they were so delighted, they sent Barnabas to help them. This was an ideal choice for Barnabas was from Cyprus, and thus understood the Greek mind. In addition, he was a Levite and was thus accepted by the Jews.

While at Antioch, Barnabas went to Tarsus—about 150 miles away by land—to find Saul. "And when he had found him, he brought him unto Antioch. And it came to pass, that a whole year they assembled themselves with the church, and taught much people" (Acts 11:26).

Where did Paul and Barnabas preach during this stay? Again, no one knows. But there are two interesting legends, mentioned by Downey. One is that they preached on a street near the Roman Pantheon. This street was called either Singon or Saigon which means "jawbone"!

The other legend expounded by the "Pseudo-Clementine Romance," written in the first part of the third century, declares that Theophilus—the one to whom Luke addressed his works—donated a "huge" house for the use of the church. These legends like so many others may or may not be true. But even if they are completely false, they do indicate what people have thought.

Up until this time, the word "Christian" had never been used. The followers of Christ had been called *believers, saints, brethren, disciples, those that call upon the name of the Lord*, and other such titles.

And now Acts 11:26 tells us: "And the disciples were called Christians first in Antioch." H. V. Morton has an interesting comment on this in his excellent book, *In the Steps of St. Paul*. "The word could not have been coined by the Jews, because they used the word Nazarene, and it is unlikely that it was applied by the Christians, for they called themselves 'saints,' 'brethren,' and 'believers.' It follows, therefore, that it was probably a word coined by a Greek, who, knowing something about the new faith, incorporated the name of Jesus Christ with those who believed in Him.

"There is further possibility that the word was used disparagingly by the Roman officials at Antioch, just as the followers of Caesar were dubbed Caesarini, of Pompey, Pempeiani, of Herod, Herodiani. If so, we may imagine that the word Christians was possibly first used by a member of the Antioch police force when he was summoned to a street in which Orthodox Jews had attacked the new sect.

" 'Those Christiani again!' he may have said, unconscious that he had made history."

During one of the meetings at Antioch, Agabus, a prophet from Jerusalem, stood up and predicted that "there should be great dearth throughout all the world" (Acts 11:28). This prediction came to pass, probably about A.D. 46. A special offering was taken and Paul and Barnabas were selected to deliver the money to Jerusalem. How the money was carried is not known, but it is quite likely that they used a letter of credit, or perhaps a traveler's check.

It is also possible that they took along a letter which explained a disagreement which the church in Antioch was having over the keeping of the law. Some of the Judaizers had contended "Except ye be circumcised after the manner of Moses, ye cannot be saved" (Acts 15:1).

The funds for famine relief were presented, and the problem about Gentiles being required to keep the law of Moses was outlined. Peter, as usual, was quick to speak. He insisted that God had "put no difference between us and them, purifying their hearts by faith. Now therefore why tempt ye God, to put a yoke upon the neck of the disciples, which neither our fathers nor we were able to bear?"(Acts 15:9,10).

The conclusion of the Jerusalem brethren was that the Gentiles should "abstain from pollutions of idols, and from fornication, and from things strangled, and from blood" (Acts 15:20). This verdict was written out and sent to Antioch "and when they had gathered the multitude together, they delivered the epistle: which when they had read, they rejoiced for the consolation" (Acts 15:30,31).

One would think that this was the end of the matter. But it was not. Paul tells us what happened in his letter to the Galatians. Galatians 2:11-16 records his words as follows: "But when Peter was come to Antioch, I withstood him to the face, because he was to be blamed. For before that certain came from James, he did eat with the Gentiles: but when they were come, he withdrew and separated himself, fearing them which were of the circumcision. And the other Jews dissembled likewise with him; insomuch that Barnabas also was carried away with their dissimulation. But when I saw that they walked not uprightly according to the truth of the gospel, I said unto Peter before them all, If thou, being a Jew, livest after the manner of Gentiles, and not as do the Jews, why compellest thou the Gentiles to live as do the Jews? We who are Jews by nature, and not sinners of the Gentiles, knowing that a man is not justified by the works of the law, but by the faith of Jesus Christ, even we have believed in Jesus Christ, that we might be justified by the faith of Christ, and not by the works of the law: for by the works of the law shall no flesh be justified."

The sharp differences between Paul and Peter and Barnabas and John Mark might have torn the church in Antioch assunder. But all of them were big men and would not allow these differences to either hinder the church or soil their mutual esteem.

It was in Antioch that Paul received his summons to do missionary work. Luke records: " . . . the Holy Ghost said, Separate me Barnabas and Saul for the work whereunto I have called them. And when they had fasted and prayed, and laid their hands on them, they sent them away" (Acts 13:2,3). And so the first missionary church was born at Antioch!

ANTIOCH

Considering how the work grew in Antioch, and how refugees from the persecution in Jerusalem fled there, the question arises: Why did these things happen in Antioch? From a merely human point of view, there is a suggested answer. The population of Antioch was perhaps three times that of Jerusalem, and the civil government seemed to have better control over Jewish mobs in Antioch than they did in Jerusalem.

The ultimate answer, of course, is that God had planned it to be this way just as He had planned for Paul to go to Philippi rather than to Bithynia. Perhaps He planned it this way because as long as the gospel was confined in its centrality to Jerusalem it might be considered a mere offshoot of Judaism—or as a *Jewish* gospel.

Before going to the next chapter, we must say a word about the other Antioch referred to in the New Testament—Pisidian Antioch. This city, north of Perga in the Roman province of Pisidia, was about three hundred miles west of the Syrian Antioch. The town had been well fortified by the Romans in order to keep peace among the neighboring tribes.

Luke tells us that Paul and Barnabas preached there on their first missionary journey (Acts 13:14). And that Paul visited it on his second and third missionary journeys (Acts 16:6 and 18:23). On the first journey, Paul preached in the synagogue, and Luke gives us a detailed account of his sermon (Acts 13:16-41). The result of this sermon was that "the next sabbath day came almost the whole city together to hear the word of God" (Acts 13:44).

This success stirred up a mob and they turned on Paul and Barnabas "and expelled them out of their coasts"(verse 50). After shaking the dust from their feet, Paul and his friend went to Iconium where they had great success and ultimately faced another mob—one that sought to stone them. From here they went to Lystra where they had so much success the crowd wanted to call Barnabas Jupiter and Paul Mercurius. But again, they faced persecution. This time, according to Acts

14:19, "And there came thither certain Jews from Antioch and Iconium who persuaded the people, and, having stoned Paul, drew him out of the city, supposing he had been dead."

Later, Paul ordained elders in Pisidian Antioch and in the neighboring towns (Acts 14:23). Some believe that Paul's letter to the Galatians was partly intended for the church in this city.

Chapter 22

Tarsus

My well-illustrated travel book on Turkey is crammed with hotel addresses, descriptions of Istanbul's nightlife, maps, menus, a money exchange table, and the lure of exotic restaurants; but nowhere in its more than two hundred pages is the city of Tarsus even mentioned. This is a pity, for its illustrious son Paul was certainly one of the half dozen most useful men who ever lived.

The Tarsus where Paul was born between A.D. 10 and 15 was at the time a city of approximately half a million. Today the population has shrunk to a mere 25,000. Nevertheless, to historians and Bible students, Tarsus, like Bethlehem, remains one of the historic cities of the world.

Located near the northeastern end of the Mediterranean, this former city of culture and learning competed with Alexandria and Rome as one of the best cities in the Empire. But had it not been for two famous passes, Tarsus would never have been even a major city.

Except for the southern front which faces the sea, this city of Paul is hedged in by the snarling teeth of two chains of jagged mountains. The snow-tipped peaks of the Tarsus range block the northern and western side of Tarsus, while the Amanus mountains block the eastern side—the side facing Syria.

Many centuries B.C.—no one knows exactly how many—engineers chiseled a pass by the side of a riverbed that crosses the Tarsus Mountains. This road which Xenophon described as being a "wagon-road, exceedingly steep and impracticable for an army to pass," was about eighty miles long. But the pass, known as the Cilician Gates, is a mere slit. The gates, however, opened the way from Tarsus to the West. On the other side, the Syrian Gates opened the way across the Amanus mountains to the East.

The Cilician Gates have a romantic history probably unequaled by any other pass. It was through them that Cyrus the Younger and his Ten Thousand marched on their way to Babylon in the summer of 401 B.C. And it was through them that Alexander the Great passed on his way to Tarsus in 333 B.C. after his great victory over the Persians on the banks of the Granicus.

When from a distance Alexander viewed the almost impossible-to-believe slit in the mountains, he feared an ambush. Remembering how the Spartans had fought at the pass of Thermopylae, he was reluctant to take a chance. And so he sent his Thracians up to the pass to see if it was protected. To his amazement, the young conqueror learned that the Persians had fled. Alexander then ordered his men forward.

Overheated because of his trek through the pass and down to Tarsus, Alexander plunged into the snow-chilled Cydnus river. Coming out of the water, he developed a sudden high fever. His physician Philip, a student of Hippocrates, mixed a medicine and assured Alexander that if he swallowed it, he could be cured.

But just as Alexander reached for the cup, he was given a frantic letter from Parmenio—one of his generals. The letter declared that Philip was in the pay of Darius and that the medicine was deadly poison. Alexander, however, was desperate. With a quick thrust of his hand he gulped down the potion and handed the message to Philip.

Alexander lived. But one wonders what would have happened if he had died and the Hellenization of the world had stopped. In that event it is probable that the New Testament would not have been written in Greek!

From Xenophon, the historian (434 B.C.?-355 B.C.?) who traveled with the Ten Thousand, we have an eyewitness description of Tarsus and the plains surrounding it as it appeared four centuries before the birth of Paul. "Thence he (Cyrus the Younger) descended to a large and beautiful plain, well-watered and full of trees of all sorts and vines; it produces an abundance of sesame, millet, wheat and barley, and it is surrounded on every side from sea to sea, by a lofty and formidable range of mountains. After descending he marched through this plain . . . to Tarsus, a large and prosperous city of Cilicia where the palace of Syennesis, the king of the Cilicians, was situated; and through the middle of the city flows a river named the Cydnus, two plethora in width. [A plethora was 97 feet, hence the river was 194 feet wide.] The inhabitants of this city had abandoned it and fled, with Syennesis, to a stronghold upon the mountains—all of them . . . except the tavern-keepers." (See Xenophon's famous book, *Anabasis*, that is, "The Expedition of Cyrus.")

In Paul's time, the city was much the same as Xenophon describes it. Only it was much larger. The Cydnus connected the city to the Mediterranean about ten miles away. As a lad, Paul must have watched the ships move up the river and unload their cargoes at the artificial docks in the midst of the city.

Some forty years before Paul's birth, Cleopatra had sailed up this river in order to meet Mark Antony. Antony had just arrived in the city after celebrating his victory over Brutus and Cassius at Philippi. And now he was annoyed at Cleopatra for having aided Cassius.

Since the Queen of Egypt did not know what awaited her, she decided to use her charms. And on that memorable day, the citizens of Tarsus saw a most unusual sight, and it is entirely possible that Paul's father was among the witnesses.

With its purple sails spread, its silver oars chunking to the rhythm of harps, flutes, and pipes, and with its gilded stern glistening in the sun, Cleopatra's ship moved majestically up the river. Cleopatra, realizing her peril, did not take chances. Having vast wealth, she used it.

Dressed in the finest silks in order to resemble Aphrodite, the goddess of love, she lounged seductively beneath an awning trimmed with gold. Fabulous jewels shimmered on her throat, wrists, and arms. Her hair, also, was decorated with jewels, and there were jewels on her fingers and hanging from her ears. And on each side of the awning, boys, dressed as cupid, fanned her with the most expensive fans the treasury of Egypt could provide.

Other ships of the fleet followed and in these were the finest entertainers, magicians, and cooks. Cleopatra knew that Antony loved Egyptian cooking and she was prepared to provide it.

Clouds of exquisite perfume were everywhere. As Antony stepped on board he must have known that he was stepping into a spider's web. But like Herod when he was enticed by Salome, he didn't care.

Undoubtedly, Paul heard this story with countless variations dozens of times; and in the years that followed, when he wrote about lust and gluttony, he must have thought about this scene.

About a mile above the city, the Cydnus tumbles over a waterfall composed of large blocks of granite. From the wild currents and mists of these falls the river flows through the city into a small lake six or seven miles below and from thence into the sea.

In Paul's day there was a wealthy suburb just north of Tarsus in the foothills. It was to this suburb that the wealthy fled during the humid summers.

Tarsus was a city of activity—and learning. Timber from the mountains was floated down on the streams and loaded into the ships that were anchored in Tarsus. Also, the city was known for its tent making. Cilician goats' hair was famous for its durability throughout the world. And this material was used for items other than tents. Perhaps Paul's cloak which he "left at Troas with Carpus" was made of this stiff material.

Rabbis had insinuated that weaving and tanning were not good occupations for Jews; but Tarsus was an independent city, and Paul did not feel bound by this prejudice. Tradition tells us that his father was a cloth merchant and a dealer in tents. Also, we are reminded of the fact that Paul, a tentmaker, was not ashamed to associate with others in the same trade— Aquila and Priscilla for example.

Tarsus was a unique crossroads of the East and the West. It had little if any anti-Semitism, and race prejudice was at a low minimum. This unique background served to help Paul develop his broad world outlook. Morally, Tarsus was a rather conservative city. In other cities, especially in Ionia, the women walked the streets in rather scanty clothes. Not so in Tarsus. Here, perhaps influenced by the Persians, the women wore veils on the streets. Some think that Paul was influenced by this custom when he wrote that a woman should wear a covering on her head as a sign that she is under man's authority (I Corinthians 11:10).

Paul, however, was here writing God's inspired word which overrode any personal prejudice, though God may have used the fact to impel Paul.

Learning in Tarsus was both a passion and a pride. Like other cities in the Empire, it had a state-supported university. Writing about this, Strabo pointed out that unlike other universities whose student body came mostly from abroad, the university in Tarsus was filled with Cilician students. Indeed, he declared that the passion to learn in Tarsus was higher than in either Athens or Alexandria.

One of the distinguished citizens of Tarsus was the Stoic philosopher Athenodorus who had passed away a decade or two before Paul's birth. He had lectured all over the world, and one of his students was Augustus Caesar. Before leaving for Athens, he had a word of caution for the Emperor. "Whenever you get angry do not say or do anything before repeating to yourself the twenty-four letters of the alphabet."

Augustus was so pleased with this advice, he invited the old man to remain with him for another year!

It was in Tarsus that Paul, or Saul as he was known in his native city, went to school. Here, he studied the Law, learned Hebrew, and was drilled in all the strictness taught by the Pharisees. Day after day, he was taught, "Don't do this! Avoid that! That is wrong! Keep the Law!"

He was probably taught to avoid Gentile learning, art, and literature. But Tarsus was such a cosmopolitan city, these things could not be completely avoided. When asked to identify himself, Paul said to the chief captain, "I am a man which am a Jew of Tarsus, a city in Cilicia, a citizen of no mean city" (Acts 21:39). In this we find an echo of the famous Greek playwright Euripides.

Paul was, of course, a Roman citizen. This citizenship was his by birth, for his parents were also citizens. Frequently in his day, high-class Jews purchased this citizenship. The price was a minimum of five hundred drachmas.

At the proper age, probably thirteen, Paul was sent to Jerusalem to study under Gamaliel—grandson of the well known Hillel. Following his conversion to Christ, Paul eventually returned to Tarsus (Acts 9:30). Here, he worked in comparative obscurity for an estimated ten years. It was while he was in Tarsus that Barnabas summoned him to help in the work at Antioch (Acts 11:25,26).

In modern Tarsus, a guide will point to a rocky cavern and claim that this is where Paul lived as a hermit during this period of waiting. But since Paul was always an active man, this is hard to accept. It is more likely that he returned to his trade, preached, and searched the Scriptures. Galatians 1:21-23 hints that during this time he did some evangelistic work.

Chapter 23

Jericho

The city of Jericho has a dozen meanings to a dozen groups—all of them different, and yet all of them romantic!

On driving into the war-scarred city, a Christian is apt to think of little Zacchaeus and the sycamore tree; an Arab might remember the day when it was an Arab stronghold; an orthodox Jew's mind would probably go back to Joshua; and an archaeologist would undoubtedly smile, considering the important discoveries made there.

Fortunately for scholars, the present Jericho is some distance from both the New Testament and the Old Testament Jericho. This means that archaeologists have been free to dig without complaints that they were ruining someone's backyard. And today a number of eminent archaeologists claim that ancient Jericho was the oldest city in the world, and that it was the lowest city on earth.

Some scholars believe that the original Jericho dates back a minimum of 5,000 years before Christ. If this date is correct, the area was inhabited at least 3,500 years before Joshua appeared on the scene!

Crouched in the scorching desert, 900 feet below sea level—
(Death Valley is only 276 feet below)—and six miles northwest
of the northern end of the Dead Sea, the city has a warm,
humid climate.

Palm-studded Jericho—it is assumed the name means
place of fragrance or moon city—has retained much of its
original character throughout the centuries. When Moses
viewed it from Mount Nebo, he referred to it as "the city of
palm trees" (Deuteronomy 34:3).

Since Jericho, on a straight line from Jerusalem is a mere
seventeen miles away, those seeking an abrupt change from
Jerusalem's 2,550-foot altitude, slip down to Jericho just as
people have done for thousands of years. This contrasting
climate has made Jericho a valuable tourist attraction from
its beginning.

The city has an excellent water supply and the soil is
extremely fertile. In addition to these assets, the background
hills rise to an altitude of 1,500 feet, thus supplying excellent
protection from an invader. Today, as one stands in the city
and views these hills, he is reminded of the words of Rahab,
spoken to the spies she had concealed. "And she said unto
them, Get you to the mountain, lest the pursuers meet you;
and hide yourselves there three days, until the pursuers be
returned: and afterward may ye go your way" (Joshua
2:16).

It was on one of these hills, Quarantania, just west of the
city, that tradition says Jesus was tempted by Satan.

The mound that now rises over the Old Testament Jericho
is known as Tell es-Sultan. Since several cities are believed to
have been built and then destroyed in this general area, scientists have named them City A, and City B, and so on.

According to John Garstang, the British archaeologist who
worked on the Jericho project from 1930 to 1936, the "late
bronze age city"—the one detroyed by Joshua—was City D.
Other scientists had already concluded that this ancient city
was surrounded by two walls: an outer wall six feet thick and

an inner wall twelve feet thick. The outer wall was estimated to have been from twenty-five to thirty feet high.

Also, a number of archaeologists were certain there was evidence that houses had been built on the inner wall. This conclusion would agree with Scripture, for Joshua 2:15 reads: "Then she let them down by a cord through the window: for her house was upon the town wall, and she dwelt upon the wall."

Garstang startled the Christian world by declaring: "The space between the two walls is filled with fragments and rubble. There are clear traces of a temendous fire, compact masses of blackened bricks, cracked stones, charred wood, and ashes. All along the walls the houses have been burned to the ground and their roofs have crashed on top of them."

Again, we have agreement with Scripture. " . . . and the people shouted with a great shout, [and] . . . the wall fell down flat . . . And they burnt the city with fire, and all that was therein" (Joshua 6:20,24).

Many have wondered how Joshua could have marched his men around the city wall in a single day. But archaeological studies show that this was entirely possible, for the complete city covered an area of only about eight acres: the size of a large mobile-home court.

The terror of the occupants of Jericho must have reached fever pitch as they watched the silent army with its priests and ark solemnly marching around the city. Their whispered conversations are reflected in what Rahab had said to the spies. "And she said unto the men, I know that the Lord hath given you the land, and that your terror is fallen upon us, and that all the inhabitants of the land faint because of you. For we have heard how the Lord dried up the water of the Red Sea for you, when ye came out of Egypt. . . . And as soon as we had heard these things, our hearts did melt, neither did there remain any more courage in any man, because of you: for the Lord your God, he is God in heaven above, and in earth beneath" (Joshua 2:9-11).

Following Garstang's work, Miss Kathleen Kenyon went to Jericho in 1952 and began to excavate. Dr. John B. Graybill, writing in the *Zondervan Pictorial Bible Dictionary* (1963), has this to say about her findings: "After seven seasons at Jericho, Miss Kenyon reports that virtually nothing remains of the Jericho of the period of Joshua (1500-1200 B.C.). The mound has suffered such denudation that almost all remains later than the third millenium B.C. have disappeared. The two walls which Garstang connected with his city D Miss Kenyon discovered to date from the third millennium, hundreds of years before the Exodus. Only a bit of pottery and possibly one building remain from the late bronze age. . . . Many scholars now believe that the Jericho of Joshua's day was little more than a fort."

The part of the building and the bit of pottery that Miss Kenyon did find, however, is of great interest. Near an ancient type oven—similar to those used by Palestinian peasants today—standing like a topless cone in the middle of the floor, there is a little jug. This bit of pottery has been dated about 1400 B.C. Concerning this, Miss Kenyon remarked, in her *Digging Up Jericho*: "The evidence seems to me to be that the small fragment of a building that we have found is part of the kitchen of a Canaanite woman, who may have dropped the juglet beside the oven and fled at the sound of the trumpets of Joshua's men."

Some archaeologists assume that the walls fell because of an earthquake. This may be. Nonetheless, it is strange that Joshua, an eyewitness, did not mention an earthquake in his report! But even though earthquakes have been credited with felling the walls and damming the Jordan, we must remember that these events happened at precisely the right time, and thus we must acknowledge the Divine intervention.

Having taken Jericho, Joshua made a solemn prophecy. "Cursed be the man before the Lord, that riseth up and buildeth this city Jericho: he shall lay the foundation thereof in his firstborn, and in his youngest son shall he set up the gates of it" (Joshua 6:26).

This prediction proved to be remarkably accurate. No one attempted to build on the ruins until the time of Ahab—some five or six hundred years later. Then Hiel attempted to do just that. The story of the subsequent disaster is noted in I Kings 16:34. Matthew Henry wrote: "He began to build in defiance of the curse well known in Israel, jesting with it perhaps as a bugbear. . . . He built for his children, but God wrote him childless; his eldest son died when he began, and the youngest when he finished, and all the rest (it is supposed) in between."

New Testament Jericho has never drawn the interest that has settled on the old city. Serious excavations did not start until 1950. But the site is of great interest; for because of the city's warm climate, the new city became a favorite place for those in power.

Mark Antony presented Jericho to Cleopatra; and she, in turn rented it to Herod the Great for a reported annual rental of $150,000. Herod had a winter palace there, and the Romans saw to it that the city was equipped with those luxuries they considered essential to the "good life." Thus, there were elaborate baths, wine cellars, vast floors tiled with mosaic, huge pictures, lively gardens, fountains, and many elaborate buildings.

It was here that Herod the Great died in 4 B.C.

Following the Moslem conquest of Palestine, Caliph Hisham Ibn Abdul built a magnificent palace for himself just north of the present Jericho. Like Herod, he loved the climate and decided on a breathtaking palace. There were enormous mosaic floors, exquisite gardens, elaborately carved fountains, rows of high, fluted columns, and fantastic pictures covering entire walls. But just as this structure—known as the Omayyad Palace—was being completed in A.D.747, an earthquake shook it down and it has never been rebuilt.

Today visitors flock to see the ruins, but there is not much left except for some floors and the remains of some walls.

Many of the ornaments and decorations can now be seen in the Rockefeller Museum in Jerusalem.

During my visit in 1958, Jericho was still in the hands of the Jordanians. But since the Six-Day War it has been governed by Israel. On my next tour in 1970, I found that the Israelis were operating an agricultural station there in order to help the Arab population make better use of the soil. Tiring of the lecture being given to us beneath the palm trees, I went out to the street. There I found that a shell had recently passed through the road sign.

When I asked an Arab about it, he said the shelling had taken place about two months before.

The lovely city of Jericho is alive with flowers, history—and sorrow. The spring of Elisha still bubbles in the center of town. As one views it, he thinks of its intriguing history as recorded in II Kings 2:21-22. Finding the spring bitter, Elisha prayed for guidance and then " . . . went forth unto the spring of the waters, and cast the salt in there, and said, Thus saith the Lord, I have healed these waters; there shall not be from thence any more death or barren land. So the waters were healed unto this day. . . . "

In the days of Jesus, Galileans making a pilgrimage to Jerusalem often went through Peraea on the east side of the Jordan in order to avoid Samaria. Those who did this, crossed over the Jordan to Jericho and from thence went to Jerusalem.

Jesus frequently visited Jericho, and while there performed a number of noted miracles. We also remember his famous parable about the man who was beaten and robbed by thieves while on his way to Jericho. The inn (that is, the inn pointed out by the smiling travel guides!), where the victim was placed by the Good Samaritan, can still be seen from the tour bus as it follows the coiling road from Jerusalem to Jericho.

Chapter 24

Bethlehem

As the Christmas season approaches, people all over the world think of Bethlehem—and especially the Christ-child. They remember the church dramas of their youth, the Christmas tree emerging from stacks of gifts and decorated with tinsel and lights, special offerings for missions, and the delightful legends of an ever-plump Santa Claus.

But what we usually forget, or never knew about Bethlehem, is that it is an ancient city with many a key role in history, and that it is also surrounded by an area that bristles with world-shaping events.

Yes, Jesus was born there. But although His birth was the most significant event in the little town's history, there were many other events which are also significant. So let us leave our comfortable room in Jerusalem and go both *down* and *up* to Bethlehem.

We go down, for Bethlehem is just a little over five miles almost due south from Jerusalem; and we go up, for Bethlehem is slightly higher than Jerusalem. All of Bethlehem, however, does not have the same height. The city rests on a limestone ridge and forms a modified semicircle with each end a shade higher than the center. The Church of the Nativity, which commemorates the place where Christ was born, and whose lead roof was once melted to make bullets, stands like a medieval fortress on the southern end of this semicircle.

Reaching out from Bethlehem, like spokes from a hub, are many historical places just a few miles away. Approximately ten miles to the north and a little to the west are the ruins of the ancient city of Gibeon. It was here that Joshua asked the Lord to cause the sun and the moon to stand still (Joshua 10:12-14). And a mere twelve miles almost due west is the site of Socoh where David confronted Goliath (I Samuel 17). Then if we go six miles to the southeast we come to the birthplace of Amos of Tekoa (Amos 1:1). And three or four miles northwest of Tekoa are the ruins of Herodium. This is the place where Herod the Great stopped the Parthians who were pursuing him from Jerusalem. Herod built a fort here, and it is also the place of his burial.

Next, by dropping fifteen miles almost due south we come to Hebron, the still-thriving city where Abraham's wife Sarah died (Genesis 23:2).

Bethlehem, sometimes referred to in the King James Version as Bethlehem-judah in order to distinguish it from another town by the same name in Zebulun, gets its name from a Hebrew and Aramaic word which means "house of bread." Today, the Arabs call it Beit Lahm, which means "house of meat."

The city is old—and distinguished. In the Bible it is first mentioned in Genesis 35:19—"And Rachel died, and was buried in the way to Ephrath, which is Beth-lehem." The Ephrath here—a variation of Ephrata, etc.—means "fruitful." A tomb alleged to be Rachel's can be seen today just north of Bethlehem on the way to Jerusalem.

The first reference to Bethlehem in the secular world is found in the Amarna letters. These letters—discovered in 1887 at El-Amarna, 190 miles south of Cairo—are from the diplomatic correspondence between Egypt and other nations.

In one of these dispatches, dated by experts to the fourteenth century B.C., it is mentioned that Bethlehem belonged to the district of "Urusalim"—Jerusalem.

Thus we have evidence that Bethlehem was flourishing well over three thousand years ago!

Christians like to remember that Bethlehem was the hometown of Boaz whose romance with Ruth is described in the Biblical book by that name. It was their son Obed who became the father of Jesse and the grandfather of David. David grew up in the neighborhood of Bethlehem; and it was in this area that he tended his father's sheep, fought the wild animals, and was eventually anointed King of Israel by the prophet Samuel. And because of this, Luke referred to the place as "the city of David, which is called Bethlehem" (Luke 2:4).

David loved the city, the surrounding Judean hills, the deep well—and the history. One has a feeling that this area is the background for the Twenty-third Psalm. And just as childhood memories bind all of us, they bound David. When Bethlehem fell temporarily under the control of a Philistine garrison, David began to remember the cool water that he used to drink at home. "Oh that one would give me drink of the water of the well of Bethlehem, that is at the gate!" he exclaimed (I Chronicles 11:17).

Impulsively, three brave men broke through the Philistine lines and brought him a drink from the well. But since they had risked their lives, David refused to drink it. Instead, "he poured it out to the Lord."

Following these events and others, Rehoboam—son of Solomon—had the city fortified in the tenth century B.C. This was done to guard the approaches to Jerusalem. He also ordered a food depot to be made there and placed the city under the command of a captain.

Some three centuries later, Micah prophesied, "But thou, Bethlehem Ephratah, though thou be little among the thousands of Judah, yet out of thee shall he come forth unto me that is to be ruler in Israel; whose goings forth have been from of old, from everlasting" (Micah 5:2).

Our next Biblical mention of Bethlehem comes from Ezra who made a listing of those who returned from the sixth century B.C. exile in Babylon. Among these, he tells us, were "an hundred twenty and three" from Bethlehem (Ezra 2:21).

The lights of Bethlehem continued to glow during succeeding centuries. The hills remained alive with sheep. Rulers came, left their marks—and were gone. There were abundant harvests, and there were occasional famines.

Then, sometime near 40 B.C., Herod the Great temporarily checked the Parthians a few miles away from the city as we have previously noted.

Thirty some years after that event—no one knows exactly how many—Joseph and Mary made the long sixty-five-mile journey from Nazareth to Bethlehem because of "a decree from Caesar Augustus, that all the world should be taxed" (Luke 2:1). (Some scholars render *taxed* as "registered" or "counted.")

It was in Bethlehem that Jesus was born and laid in "a manger; because there was no room for them in the inn" (Luke 2:7). And it was here that the wise men came (Matthew 2:1-11).

Thus the prophecies of Micah, Isaiah, and many others were fulfilled. God had pinpointed Bethlehem to be the place where His only begotten Son would be born, and His will was accomplished.

But Bethlehem was still to remain in the current news. Alarmed at the inquiries from the wise men about the birth of the King of the Jews, Herod gathered all the chief priests and scribes together and demanded where this one should be born. They quoted for him the prophecy from Micah. The place was Bethlehem. Perhaps remembering his previous struggle near Bethlehem, Herod decided to kill the new-born king at once. Matthew tells us that Herod "slew all the children that were in Bethlehem, and in all the coasts thereof, from two years old and under" (Matthew 2:16).

As far as we know, no church or shrine was built over the traditional "manger" until Constantine built the Church of the

Nativity in the first part of the fourth century A.D. But how was he to know the actual spot where Jesus was born? Accurate records were not kept in those days.

Constantine found a way. After the Roman Emperor Hadrian (A.D. 76-138) rebuilt Jerusalem and changed its name to Aelia Capitolina, he systematically destroyed the places venerated by Christians. Over what he believed to be Golgotha, he built a temple to Venus. Over the stable in Bethlehem he built a temple to Adonis—the handsome youth of Greek mythology who, according to Roman legend, fell in love with the goddess Aphrodite. With the place of Christ's birth thus marked, Constantine tore down the pagan building and replaced it with a church.

At various times there were at least three doors to this Church of the Nativity built at the same spot. Now there is only one and it is extremely low. As I stood outside to take a picture, I heard the guide warn, "Don't bump your head." Nevertheless, three people in a row did just that as they entered. The reason for the low entrance is not so that people will have to bow their heads in homage as they enter, as some have assumed. No, it is for a more practical reason than that.

During the many feuds that have scarred Bible lands, there were times when enemies of Christ rode right into the building on horses and donkeys in order to disturb the worshipers. Now such disturbance is impossible. Evidence of two previous doorways can still be seen.

Within a century or two after the construction of the Church of the Nativity, it was almost completely destroyed. But it was rebuilt by the Christian emperor Justinian in the Sixth century. One guide assured me that the sturdy Corinthian pillars of dull red stone in the present building are those of Constantine. Some even insist that a few of the pillars were rescued from Hadrian's temple.

In the fifteenth century, decades before Columbus lifted his anchors, King Edward IV of England donated a new roof for the church. The English oak beams and several tons of lead were sent in care of Venetian shippers. They unloaded these supplies at the port of Jaffa—the Biblical Joppa from which Jonah sailed.

How long these beams stayed in place, no one knows. But it is said that the roof was melted down by the Turks and turned into bullets for use in their war against the Venetians.

The most interesting spot in the building is the stable. However, stables in Palestine in the days of Jesus were not separate buildings as one might suppose. Instead, the stable— often a cave—was connected to the inn for the convenience of travelers arriving with animals. To reach the stable cave at Bethlehem one must decend two flights of stairs in the church. And there, behind a curtain fringing the top of the cave is a silver star imbedded in marble. Around this star is the inscription *Hic de Virgine Maria Jesus Christus Natus Est*—"Here Jesus Christ is born of the Virgin Mary."

A little over one hundred years ago this star was removed, and the removal led to a quarrel between France and Russia that finally escalated into the Crimean War where many thousands were killed.

It was here that Jerome made his remarkable translation work which ultimately became the Vulgate—a translation of the Bible that is still used by the Roman Catholic Church. The place where he worked is now a wing of the church. Nearby is an altar erected in honor of the "Holy Innocents"—the children killed by the order of Herod in his attempt to kill Jesus.

Bethlehem is no longer the "little town" Phillips Brooks visited. This city of David has become the triple town of Bethlehem-Beit Jala Sahur and has a combined population in excess of 27,000 of which 14,400 are nominal Christians. The rest are Moslem. In Bethlehem alone, however, Christians are slightly outnumbered by Moslems.

While walking around Bethlehem, one is apt to see a number of blue eyes. The reason? Simple. There was a time centuries ago when the city overflowed with Crusaders. Ah, but that's another story.

Chapter 25

Jerusalem

The information available about Jerusalem is utterly enormous—and easily accessible. According to the Talmud, "When the world was created, it received ten measures of beauty. Nine fell on Jerusalem . . . one on the rest of the earth." Thus, to deal with any single aspect, one would require an entire volume.

Since this is the case, we will not write about the city's colorful beginnings, its complex changes across the centuries, nor the many times it has been destroyed. Instead, we shall write about the tomb of Christ and the Temple—now replaced by the Dome of the Rock. Curiously, much of this material is unknown to evangelical Christians. And this is a pity, for these places are visited by millions every year.

While in Jerusalem on vacation from his campaigns in China, General Charles Gordon was directed by a guide to the Church of the Holy Sepulcher—the alleged burial place and the site of the crucifixion of Jesus Christ. Gordon listened with qualified interest as the eager guide explained the story of the church. It seemed that until the year A.D. 325, neither the site of the empty tomb nor the crucifixion of Jesus had been located. During that year Bishop Macarius of Jerusalem attended the Council of Nicea. While there, he mentioned this fact to Constantine and suggested that the historic spot was probably under Hadrian's Temple of Venus.

Constantine ordered Macarius to have the temple removed and to make a search. This was done in A.D. 326. The empty tomb, according to the story, and there are many variations, was found beneath the debris. Excited by this discovery, Constantine decreed that a place of prayer be erected on the spot that would "be worthy of the most wonderful place in the world."

Forthwith, the Church of the Holy Sepulcher was built of stone. This building was destroyed and rebuilt several times during the following fifteen hundred years. Still, it is seriously claimed that a certain portion of it remains a part of the original church. But as Gordon viewed the shrine in 1883, he was vaguely dissatisfied. Perhaps some of this uneasiness was because of the amount of gold that had been used in order to "make it worthy." Most of all, however, he was unhappy because the Church of the Holy Sepulcher stands *within* the present walls of Jerusalem, while Hebrews 13:12 states that he "suffered *without* the gate."

Having almost a year of free time to spend in Jerusalem, Gordon began to search for a more suitable site. General Gordon, commonly called Chinese Gordon, was one of the most colorful men who ever lived. He distinguished himself in China where he helped to take Peking, fought in many other parts of the world, and served as Governor of Sudan. He was an extremely eccentric person, and his eccentricities took many forms. In China, he insisted that his salary be reduced from £3,200 per year to £1,200 per year, and he spent 80 percent of this on medicines and comforts for his men. When the Prince of Wales invited him for lunch, he refused the invitation on grounds that he went to bed at 9:30! But he got things done, and all of England knew it.

With Bible in hand, Gordon searched all around Jerusalem

for a probable spot that could be identified with the Crucifixion. He was wearying from this search when suddenly he noticed a cream-colored cliff from his hotel window. As he studied the wall-like bluff, two hollow eyes and then a portion of a nose seemed to leap out at him. A moment later, it seemed that he was staring at a skull. Leafing quickly to Mark 15:22, he read: "And they bring him unto the place Golgotha, which is, being interpreted, The place of a skull."

Excitedly, he hurried over to the cliff and studied some more. The cliff, he noticed, was just outside the Damascus Gate. This agreed with the passage in Hebrews, that Christ suffered without (outside) the gate. Then in John 19:41 he read: "Now in the place where he was crucified there was a garden; and in the garden a new sepulchre, wherein was never man yet laid." This clearly meant that if the cliff was the authentic place there would be an ancient tomb nearby. Gordon went to work immediately. Soon he located a tomb that had been discovered by a Greek in 1867. The tomb was only a few yards from those haunting eyes!

But again he insisted on checking with the New Testament. This time he was fascinated with Mark 15:40: "There were also women looking on afar off. . . . " Thinking of the crowds that watched the crucifixion, and remembering women are usually shorter than men, he decided that if they had seen him from "afar off" the cross would have had to have been on an elevated place.

This reasoning quickened his pulse a trifle more.

Next, he began to question local people. From them he learned that there was a widely circulated legend that in ancient times criminals were frequently tossed to their deaths from those cliffs. He also learned that local Arabs called the place El-Heidemiyeh—The Rent. Thoughts of the rent reminded him of the earthquake that shook the land during the crucifixion.

Thoroughly convinced that he had found the actual place, Gordon drew detailed sketches and mailed them to Sir John

E. Cowell, Controller of the Household of Buckingham Palace. Soon, interested people united and made an appeal through the *Times* for two thousand pounds with which to purchase the land containing the tomb.

The funds were raised and the land was secured. But is the place authentic? No one really knows, and serious doubts are beginning to emerge. Excavations in Jerusalem by Miss Kathleen Kenyon in 1963 indicate the possibility of another wall. This Second Wall—mentioned by Josephus—may have placed the land occupied by the Church of the Holy Sepulcher *outside* the walls. Moreover, it is quite unreasonable to assume that Bishop Macarius did not know the passage in Hebrews which says that "he suffered without the gate."

Others, however, strongly believe that the cream-colored cliff is the authentic place. Lord Elton, Gordon's biographer, wrote, in *Gordon of Khartoum*: "Gordon was not quite the first to maintain that the Skull Hill . . . was the true site of the crucifixion; at least four writers before Gordon, among them Renan in his *Vie de Jesus*, had championed the theory. But it was the knowledge that it had been endorsed by Gordon which first gained it wide acceptance in Britain and North America."

Rider Haggard, a distinguished novelist whose life covered the period of "discovery," wrote: "Now as it chances, on the cliff at this spot, believed to be the Place of Stoning, and by many that of the crucifixion, the face of the rock, looking toward Jerusalem, has undoubtedly a fantastic, but, to my fancy, a very real resemblance to a rotting human skull. . . . There is the low corroded forehead; there are two deep hollows that make the eyes; there is something which might be the remnant of a nose, and beneath, near to the ground level, a suggestion of twisted and decaying lips. . . . If two thousand years ago, the face of the cliff was approximately as it appears today, may not some fanciful-minded Jews have caught this likeness and designated it on that account, 'The Place of a Skull'? If so, in view of its traditions and horrible use, the name would have been likely to cling to the site from age to age."

The first time I visited the Garden Tomb—the new name for Gordon's Calvary—it was being kept by Dr. S. J. Mattar, an Arab refugee. Slightly bald, and with a trim moustache, he was garbed in casual western clothes. He and his wife invited me to dinner; and while I waited he showed me around. A thorough Christian, he was one of the most gentle men I have ever met. Unfortunately, during the Six Day War, while he and his wife were hiding in the Empty Tomb, he decided to make a dash for his house to get something. Just outside the Tomb, he was cut down by a trigger-happy Israeli soldier.

The lovely garden of that day has since been improved. Today there are exquisite walks, stone bridges, and benches placed in strategic places for the thousands of tourists who come to meditate and to pray. Many flowers mentioned in the Bible have been planted. There are low hedges of rosemary, brilliant patches of geraniums, tall, shady pines, and large fields of carefully tended grass.

As the years go by, more and more people fall in love with the place, and more and more things show up to increase one's belief in the garden's authenticity. For example, some years ago a number of distinguished archaeologists were asked to examine the tomb. After considerable study, they agreed that it dates back to the time of Herod the Great.

Then in 1952, the keepers began to have trouble with the cistern. While it was being repaired, the workers discovered that it was much larger than it had been previously supposed. Indeed, it was 56 by 33 feet and the distance from the floor to the ceiling was 36 feet—making it a rather large cistern. In addition to the startling size, a cross was found embedded in one of the walls and secured with Roman cement. This could indicate that the place had been used by a congregation for Christian worship. Could it be that this spot was chosen because of its proximity to the Garden Tomb? Perhaps!

And even more recently, a winepress was found near the tomb. Such a press might indicate that the garden was a flower garden used by a wealthy person such as Joseph of Arimathea who allowed the body of Jesus to be placed in his own personal tomb. It also reminds us of the prophetic words of Isaiah: "I have trodden the winepress alone" (Isaiah 63:3).

Authentic or not, the Garden Tomb is the "must" of all visitors in Jerusalem; and although I have been there several times, when I return to Jerusalem, that is the first place I plan to visit.

To the average tourist the second most interesting place in Jerusalem is the Dome of the Rock, incorrectly called the Mosque of Omar. As Christians advance toward this mosque on the eastern end of the Street of the Chain, many are reminded of the words of Jesus: "And Jesus went out, and departed from the temple: and his disciples came to him for to shew him the buildings of the temple. And Jesus said unto them, See ye not all these things? verily I say unto you, There shall not be left here one stone upon another, that shall not be thrown down" (Matthew 24:1,2).

At the time of this conversation, the new temple—commonly called Herod's Temple—started in 20-19 B.C., was only in the midst of construction. Indeed, it was not finished until A.D. 64—a quarter of a century after the crucifixion of Jesus! And even at that time there was some finishing work which the builders planned to do.

Altogether, Herod's Temple occupied approximately twenty-six acres. Upon viewing it, Josephus was overwhelmed. He wrote: "It is the most prodigious work that was ever heard of by man."

But the building the tourist sees is not this one; for, just as Jesus had prophesied, in A.D. 70 Herod's Temple was destroyed and it was never rebuilt. And the fact that it was not rebuilt is quite remarkable, for the Roman emperor, known as Julian the Apostate, determined to do just that. Edward Gibbon wrote: "The restoration of the Jewish temple was secretly connected with the ruin of the Christian church." Julian's efforts were frustrated by "an earthquake, a whirl-

195

wind, and a fiery eruption." (See *The Decline and Fall of the Roman Empire.*)

After Titus had destroyed Jerusalem, the city remained in ruins. And then, incensed by the Jews, Hadrian completely destroyed the city in A.D. 135. He even ordered the ruins to be obliterated. After this was done, he rebuilt the city on Roman lines and named it Aelia Capitolina. In addition, he decreed that no Jew could enter the city except on special occasions. Violators were crucified. However, Christians were allowed to remain.

From this time on until A.D. 635 the site of the Temple remained desolate. And remembering the prophecy of Jesus, many Christians rejoiced. Also, they decided to see to it that the Temple was never rebuilt. In their campaign to do this, they piled sewage over the rubble. This thought spread throughout the Empire; and pious Christians, hoping to further the obliteration of the Temple, brought their refuse from as far away as Constantinople! Thus, Mount Moriah became a dunghill.

The only part of the Temple that was not destroyed was a western retaining wall, now popularly known as the Wailing Wall. This Western Wall—the name preferred by the Israelis—attracts Jews from all over the world. The stones in the wall date back to Herod. Today, Jews stand before these massive stones while they read favorite passages from the Old Testament and offer up prayers. In addition, they write out prayers and wedge them between the stones. As they pray, they remember how the power of the Lord filled the Temple after it had been completed by Solomon. "And it came to pass, when the priests were come out of the holy place, that the cloud filled the house of the Lord, So that the priests could not stand to minister because of the cloud: for the glory of the Lord had filled the house of the Lord" (I Kings 8:10,11).

But Solomon's magnificent Temple lasted for less than four hundred years. It was burned in 587 B.C. by Nebuzaradan—Nebuchadnezzar's general—eleven years after King

Jehoiachin had been taken captive to Babylon.

The next Temple was built in 516 B.C. and is known as Zerubbabel's Temple. Because of this, one would think that Herod's Temple was the third one. But Jews insist that Herod merely rebuilt and enlarged Zerubbabel's Temple, and that his—the last one—was the Second Temple!

Let us, however, forget the Temple for a moment and step into the Dome of the Rock. Inside, we meet Christians, Moslems, and Jews, for all of these groups have a common heritage in the place. The first thing that takes our attention is the huge bare rock with a hole piercing its center. It is firmly claimed that on this rock—Moriah— Abraham planned to sacrifice his son Issac. Moslems also insist that at one time the Ark of the Covenant rested on it, and that it was on this stone that Mohammed mounted his mare el-Burak and made his "Night-Journey" to heaven. According to Moslem legend, this horse had eagle wings, a man's head, and a human voice.

To Christians, the whole area is important, for Jesus often frequented the Temple and taught many a lesson there. Also, when the people took stones to throw at Him, "Jesus hid himself, and went out of the temple, going through the midst of them, and so passed by" (John 8:59).

But the fact that this place is a mosque rather than a church or a temple, plunges us into history again. Up until Jerusalem fell to the Moslems, the whole Temple area was desolate. After the fall, Patriarch Sophronius, the one who represented Jerusalem, met the conquering general, Caliph Omar, on the Mount of Olives in order to arrange terms.

"Verily, you are assured," said Omar, "of the complete security of your lives, your goods, and your churches, which will not be inhabited nor destroyed by Moslems." Following this promise, he dressed in rags and followed Sophronius back to Jerusalem. Soon it was time for Moslems to pray. The Patriarch took him to the church of the Holy Sepulcher. But Omar refused to pray there.

"If I had prayed inside the church thou wouldst have lost it," he said. "The believers would have taken it from thee, saying 'Omar prayed here.' " And this undoubtedly was true, for Omar was Islam's second caliph, having followed no other than Abu Bakr, Mohammed's father-in-law!

Sophronius took him to various churches but he would have nothing to do with them. Finally, he led the way to the ancient Temple area and showed Omar the location of the rock known as Moriah. Delighted, Omar ceremoniously cleared away some of the dung with his own hands. After the stone had been cleared by workers, he had a wooden mosque built over it.

Jerusalem was now a Moslem city and its name was changed to El-Kuds (The Holy). El-Kuds was then considered the third most sacred city in Islam, Mecca being first and Medina second. For an entire generation Omar's wooden building seemed to satisfy the people. But in A.D. 687, Mecca being in enemy hands, Abd-el-Malik, caliph of Damascus, decided to make El-Kuds the number one city. Because of this decision, he ordered the Dome of the Rock to be built.

At this time there were no Arab architects capable of fulfilling his wishes, and so like Solomon who had employed outsiders to help build the First Temple, the caliph employed Hellenized Syrians. These men produced a masterpiece. And today the Dome of the Rock is the best of that type of architecture in existence. The building has been carefully repaired from time to time, and in these repairs one can see the stamp of history—and human nature!

Hoping to add glory to his name, an imposter wrote in large letters in the inner arcade: "This Qubbat was built by the servant of Allah, Abdullah al-Imam, The Prince of believers, Al-Ma'moon, in the year 72 AH, may Allah accept this and be pleased with him. Amen." This inscription was written in Arabic over the erased name of the real planner of the building: Abd-el-Malik. Curiously the glory-seeker did not change the date, and thus his hypocrisy is clearly apparent.

"AH" means "After the Hegira"—Mohammed's flight from Mecca to Medina. This flight occured on July 16, 622. The year one in the Moslem calendar starts on July 1 of that year.

The Moslems claim that there is a gold chest within this mosque which contains two of Mohammed's whiskers. Whether this is true or not, Mecca remains the number one city in the Moslem world and Jerusalem a mere number three. The number two spot goes to Medina.

During the Crusades when Jerusalem was occupied by the Crusaders, the Dome of the Rock was used as a Christian church building. A cross was placed on top of the dome and the big rock was covered with marble and fenced in. The fence was necessary because Christian pilgrims insisted on chipping the stone for souvenirs. These chips, it is said, were worth their weight in gold.

The cross remained on the dome for less than a century, for Jerusalem was retaken by Saladin in 1187. Today the Dome of the Rock is within the jurisdiction of Israel. Nevertheless, it is still under the direct control of the Moslems, and sometimes they will not allow tourists to enter it. The Dome of the Rock remains one of the most interesting buildings in the world. It overflows with mystery, romance, and even intrigue; and to trace all the tales associated with it—many given with a shrug and a smile—would require a dozen lifetimes.

Chapter 26

Nazareth

Having seen Jerusalem and Bethlehem, almost every tourist is eager to go north and visit Nazareth—the boyhood town of Jesus. But having looked around the city, many are vaguely disappointed.

The cave with its carpenter shop above where Jesus allegedly lived with Mary and Joseph seems quite unreal, and one is also tempted to doubt the authenticity of the Church of the Annunciation. It is claimed that this building was erected over the home of Mary's parents, and that it was here Gabriel announced to the startled teenager that she would conceive a child by the Holy Ghost and that His name would be Jesus.

There are places in Nazareth, however, that seem very real. For example, there is Mary's Well, also called the Virgin's Fountain. During the boyhood of Jesus, this was the city's main water supply. And as He spoke to the Samaritan woman about "a well of water springing up into everlasting life" (John 4:14), His mind must have gone back to those days when His mother Mary filled her jug with water for the family.

The old city of Nazareth with its quaint carpenter shops,

noisy children, flat roofs, green cypress trees, and low hills has seemingly not changed since Jesus walked its dusty streets. Still, one has serious questions. The paved streets, numbered houses, overhead wires make a difference as do also the sputtering automobiles and the glass windows in the shops and homes. In addition, it is an Arab city with an Arab mayor. I am certain that if Joseph were suddenly resurrected, he would blink a few times before he recognized where he was.

But there is one thing that has not changed much across the centuries: and this is the general topography of the land. And in this topography there remains a vital and extremely important story.

An efficiency expert might wonder why Jesus was conceived in Nazareth if He, to fulfill prophecy, was to be born in Bethlehem. Today, the sixty-five air miles from Nazareth to Bethlehem seem insignificant; but as Mary, great with child, made the journey it was a long, long trip—a trip that took several torturous days. Had He been conceived in Bethlehem or even Jerusalem such a trip would have been quite unnecessary.

Undoubtedly God had many reasons, and perhaps one of them was that He wanted to confirm to the world that He delights in doing mysterious things. Both Bethlehem and Jerusalem are mentioned many times in the Old Testament; but search as one will from Genesis through Malachi, one will not find a single reference to Nazareth. Moreover, New Testament Nazareth had a scurrilous reputation. It was the kind of town that caused Roman soldiers to smirk if they had a day or two to spend there. And all of us remember the words of Nathanael who exclaimed: "Can there any good thing come out of Nazareth?" (John 1:46).

Nazareth—now called en-Natzirah—is perched on a hill within a cup formed by surrounding hills. These hills shut off the main view. But by climbing the rim and looking south, the Plain of Esdraelon—also called the Valley of Jezreel—stretches out to the dim hills of Samaria.

These plains encompass at least twenty battlefields. From them swirled the dust stirred by the chariots of Egypt, Assyria, and Babylon. It was here Deborah defeated the Canaanites; and it was here that Saul and his three sons fell in their battle with the Philistines.

A glance at a topographical map of Palestine shows that the Plain of Esdraelon nearly cuts the country from the west of the Jordan River to the Mediterranean into two sections. And from the rim south of Nazareth, one can almost see two eras.

To the south, toward Jerusalem, one sees the Old Testament era; and toward the north, one sees Nazareth, Galilee, and other places made famous in the New Testament era. In the *must* book, *In the Steps of the Master*, H. V. Morton says: "Everyone must feel how different are these two worlds. In the New Testament we seem to have emerged from a dark, fierce Eastern world into a clear light that is almost European. The center of the Old Testament world is rigid, exclusive Jerusalem; the center of the New Testament world is Galilee, a country crossed in the time of Christ by the great military roads from the north and by the ancient caravan routes from the east."

This contrast between "New Testament" Galilee and "Old Testament" Judea is made even more sharp when we realize that Nazareth is less than twenty miles from the ever-fresh Sea of Galilee, while Jerusalem is approximately the same distance from the ever-dead Dead Sea. But at the same time we must keep in mind that both sections are connected by the Jordan River!

Jesus was conceived in New Testament Nazareth, but He was born in Old Testament Bethlehem. He grew up in New Testament Nazareth and chose His disciples—with the exception of Judas—in New Testament Galilee. But He was crucified and resurrected in Old Testament Jerusalem.

Also, Jesus preached in Old Testament Jerusalem, but most of His ministry was in New Testament Galilee. The two sections, in many ways, were separate, and yet in other ways they were combined. Was all of this planned by God, or are we reading something into the map and history that is not intended? It is an intriguing question. But here are some facts.

After Joseph and Mary had fled to Egypt because of their fear of Herod, they learned that Herod was dead. They then decided to return to Judea. "But when he [Joseph] heard that Archelaus did reign in Judea in the room of his father Herod, he was afraid to go thither ... He turned aside into the parts of Galilee: And he came and dwelt in a city called Nazareth: that it might be fulfilled which was spoken by the prophets, He shall be called a Nazarene" (Matthew 2:22,23).

Following His temptation near Jericho in Judea, Jesus returned to Nazareth. And there "he went into the synagogue on the sabbath day, and stood up for to read. And there was delivered unto him the book of the prophet Esaias. And when he had opened the book, he found the place where it was written, The Spirit of the Lord is upon me, because he hath anointed me to preach the gospel to the poor; he hath sent me to heal the brokenhearted, to preach deliverance to the captives, and recovering of sight to the blind, to set at liberty them that are bruised, To preach the acceptable year of the Lord" (Luke 4:16-19).

After Jesus had finished reading, He closed the book, handed it to the minister and said: "This day is this scripture fulfilled in your ears" (verse 21).

Angry because of what Jesus had claimed, they rose up "and thrust him out of the city, and led him unto the brow of the hill whereon their city was built, that they might cast him down headlong. But he passing through the midst of them went his way" (Luke 4:29,30).

Today, this place where they wanted to throw Jesus from the cliff is known as the Hill of Precipitation. Some of this hill is disappearing, for the Israelis are quarrying rock from it to be used in building projects.

But in spite of this rejection, Jesus remained for a time in Galilee. From Nazareth He went to Capernaum, "A city of Galilee," and there He began to assemble the Twelve. The debate will never be settled, but there are some who feel that Jesus was rejected from Nazareth a second time. The second occasion is recorded in Matthew 13, where Jesus, when He had finished speaking to the people in parables from the boat, left them and went to His "own country," presumably to His own hometown of Nazareth. There He taught in their synagogue. The people were offended at His teaching and scoffed at Him.

After each of these incidents—assuming that there were two—Jesus said: "A prophet is not without honour, save in his own country, and in his own house" (Matthew 13:57; see also Luke 4:24). But although the saying is true, Jesus never forgot Nazareth!

The dramatic connection between Nazareth and Jerusalem had an unusual exposure in 1878. At that time, a slab of marble with an inscription on it, found in Nazareth, was sent to a German collector of antiquarian items. Froehner, the collector, apparently saw nothing unusual about the inscription. But after it was given to the Louvre in 1930, a noted historian, Michel Medailles, was startled by what he read and published his findings in 1932.

The inscription, according to his translation, says "Ordinance of Caesar. It is my pleasure that graves and tombs remain undisturbed in perpetuity for those who have made them for the cult of their ancestors, or children or members of their house. If, however, any man lay information that another has either demolished them, or has in any other way extracted the buried, or has maliciously transferred them to other places in order to wrong them, or had displaced the sealing or other stones, against such a one I order that a trial be instituted, as in respect of the gods, so in regard to the cult of mortals. For it shall be much more obligatory to honor the buried. Let it be absolutely forbidden for anyone to disturb them. In the case of contravention I desire that the offender be sentenced to capital punishment on the charge of violation of sepulture."

The exciting thing about the find is that it tends to emphasize the belief of the early Christians in the resurrection of Jesus Christ. Scholars believe that this law was made by the Roman Emperor Claudius around A.D. 50. It was a year before this that Claudius expelled the Jews from Rome (see Acts 18:1-2). Although considered a fool by many, Claudius was actually an accomplished scholar and his writings fill many a volume. He was angry at the Jews, and according to Suetonius, "the Jews at Rome caused continuous disturbances at the instigation of Chrestus." Because of this "he expelled them from the city."

Could it be that Claudius was convinced that the Jews were especially energetic because of their belief in the resurrection of Christ, their leader? Yes, that is entirely possible. And this belief may have inspired his edict. Perhaps he was afraid the Christiani might try to contrive another resurrection. But why was the slab found in Nazareth, when Jesus was resurrected in Jerusalem?

Once again, no one knows. But in God's plan, Nazareth and Jerusalem do seem to have a mysterious connection, much in the way the Old and the New Testaments have a mysterious relationship as we study them.

Chapter 27

A Look at the People

It is only natural for us now to pause and ask: What was life like for the common people—people like you and me—who lived in the cities and under the rulers of this amazing world of the early Christians?

In comparison to our computerized, drug-edged, wife-employed world, it seems—at least on the surface—that the New Testament world was an extremely simple one. But this is a false assumption.

True, the New Testament world didn't have radio, electricity, television, the simple compass, telescopes, movable type, nuclear physics, or combustion engines. Also, the entire Mediterranean world enjoyed the *Pax Romana*—Roman peace. (This peace, beginning with Augustus Caesar, existed because no country was daring enough to risk war with Rome.)

Pax Romana meant that a Roman citizen could go anywhere within the Empire without a passport and with the knowledge that the Empire would defend him wherever he might be. Nonetheless, the New Testament world seethed with problems. For one thing it was multilingual. Anyone who could only speak and read one language was a severely handicapped person.

When Jesus was crucified, the sign dictated by Pilate which topped the cross, JESUS OF NAZARETH THE KING OF THE JEWS, was written in Hebrew, Latin, and Greek. Moreover, each language used a different set of characters to write those words. Then, as Jesus was dying, He spoke in Aramaic—a fourth language. And even more languages than these were used on the Day of Pentecost.

In addition to diverse languages in the New Testament world, there were diverse calendars. Had a Roman soldier written to his wife in Rome about the Crucifixion, he would have dated his letter *Aprilis*, 784 A.U.C. A Jew, on the other hand, would have dated his letter, *Nisan*, 3790.

The A.U.C. used by the Romans stood for *Ab Urbe Condita*, "from the founding of the City," the mythical date of the founding of Rome in 753 B.C. The Jewish year went back to *creation*!

The Jewish year was a lunar one—that is, it consisted of twelve complete phases of the moon. But since it takes the moon only 29 1/2 days to complete its phases, twelve of them only equaled 354 days. In contrast to this, the calendar authorized by Julius Caesar in 46 B.C., followed the solar system—the time it takes the spinning world to go completely around the sun, which is 365 1/4 days.

Julius Caesar's calendar was divided into twelve months of 30 and 31 days alternately except for February which was assigned 29 days. All of this was simple enough, but there were two main complications. One, since the Romans had been following the shorter lunar year of 354 days, the seasons were out of sequence. And in order to make up for this, the year 46 B.C., known as the *year of confusion*, was fifteen months long. 45 B.C., however, started on January 1, and was twelve months, 365 days, long.

Thankful for this improvement, the Romans changed the name of their fifth month, *Quintilis*, to July in honor of Julius Caesar. Ah, but this caused problem number two. When

Augustus Caesar came along it seemed only fair that one of the months should be named after him. This was done by renaming the sixth month, *Sextilis*, August, in his honor. Still, this did not seem to be quite fair, for Julius Caesar's month, July, had 31 days, and the new August had only 30 days. But the solution was simple: one day was snitched out of February, reducing it to 28 days, and added to August, giving it 31 days!

Studying the Julian Calendar in our time, we wonder why July our seventh month, was named after Quintilis, the fifth month; and why August, our eighth month, was named after Sextilis, their sixth month. The answer is that the Roman calendar, prior to the Julian Calendar, started with March. Indeed, March was the first month of the English year until the middle 1700s!

In spite of the Julian Calendar, pious Jews retained their lunar calendar. But since this calendar upset their seasons due to the time lag, the rabbis had a problem. Passover was celebrated on the 14th of Nisan, and for this celebration the earliest ears of barley had to be ready for the feast.

To remedy the time lag, a thirteenth month, *Veadar*, was occasionally slipped into the cycle. But the Samaritans refused to recognize the extra month when it was decreed in Jerusalem. Instead, they named one to suit themselves.

And in addition to the above confusion, many Greek cities insisted on following a calendar brought to them by Alexander the Great!

(The A.D. and B.C. system of our time was born through the efforts of Dionysius Exiguus, a monk who journeyed to Rome slightly after A.D. 525. Given the task of splitting the centuries into *Before Christ* and *Anno Domini*, he made use of several New Testament signposts including the rule of Augustus Caesar. Unfortunately, he made at least two mistakes. He forgot to count the four years that Augustus Caesar ruled as Octavian, and to remember that Jesus had been born *before* the death of Herod the Great. Because of these mistakes, we know that Jesus was born between 4 and 7 B.C.!)

As confusing as the languages and calendars were, money was fairly simple. Today, a tourist traveling throughout the former Roman Empire has to deal with various types of money and contend with money changers on the way. Also, some of the paper money that passes through his hands may be so worn and repaired he has to be careful with it. This was not the case during the reign of the Caesars!

Although there were traveler's checks in New Testament times, paper money had not been invented. Roman coins were honored throughout the Empire. Coins had on them the stamp of the Caesars and were used for propaganda purposes. For example, when Julius Caesar adopted his nephew Octavian, he informed the world by minting a special coin. Julius Caesar's head was on one side and Octavian's head was on the other side. After an earthquake leveled twelve Asiatic cities, Roman mints gushed with a new coin. The reverse side of this coin showed Tiberius on the throne surrounded by the words CIVITATIBUS ASIAE RESTITUTIS, translated essentially: "Upon the reconstruction of the cities of Asia."

Roman coins were accepted throughout the Roman Empire, but they were not allowed in the Jewish Temple in Jerusalem. The reason for this is because of the images on Roman coins, and Exodus 20:4 is extremely plain: "Thou shalt not make unto thee any graven image, or any likeness of any thing that is in heaven above, or that is in the earth beneath, or that is in the water under the earth."

Since coins with images on them were not allowed in the Temple, money changers did a lively business in providing worshipers with Temple currency. But they were limited to a silver *meah* on each transaction.

Roman money, like all money, depreciated in value across the centuries. Originally, an *as* consisted of a full pound of copper. But by 241 B.C. it only weighed two ounces, then by 202 B.C. it had slipped to a mere half an ounce. This depreciation continued, and by A.D. 60 it only weighed a quarter of an ounce.

A LOOK AT THE PEOPLE

The history of the *denarius*—penny—is equally as dramatic. Nero reduced the silver content of this coin to ninety percent, Trajan to eighty-five percent, Aurelius to seventy-five, Commodus to seventy, and Septimius Severus (A.D. 146-211) to fifty percent.

Interest rates, too, were constantly changing. During the reign of Augustus, the rate was a modest four percent; but after his death the rate went to six percent, and by the time of Constantine (272-337) the rate had soared to the legal limit— twelve percent! The Roman Government in New Testament times tried to control the economy by varying interest rates just as governments do in our times. This can be verified by considering the panic of A.D.33.

Augustus Caesar, with his heart set on turning Rome into a city of marble, kept the mints busy stamping out money. He was a lavish spender, and very clever at dreaming up new forms of taxes. Readers of the New Testament remember Luke 2:1, "And it came to pass in those days, that there went out a decree from Caesar Augustus, that all the world should be taxed."

Tiberius, however, was an extremely thrifty man. He believed in economy and balanced budgets. He restricted the issue of money. Indeed, his treasury managed to hoard 2,700,000,000 sesterces. The result of this thrift was that inflation was replaced by deflation. Soon, there was a series of bankruptcies. Banks closed. Interest rates soared. At this point, Tiberius came up with a most unusual solution: He, according to Will Durant in *Caesar and Christ*, distributed "100,000,000 sesterces to the banks, to be lent without interest for three years on the security of realty."

This move forced money lenders to lower their rates, and eventually prosperity came back to the Empire.

Due to the mortality rate of children, the average length of life in ancient Rome was only 25 years! A basic reason for this was because the Romans accepted the dogmas of Aristotle (384-322 B.C.) This famous Greek wrote: " . . . the justice of a master or a father is a different thing from that of a citizen, *for a son or slave is property, and there can be no injustice to one's own property"* (italics added).

Accepting this dogma, deformed or unwanted children were thrown out in the snow, or even on refuse dumps where they might either be rescued or devoured by wild animals. This destruction of infants continued until the time of Constantine.

The Romans were extremely fond of medicine, and doctors were held in such high regard that Augustus exempted them from taxes. Also, they charged high fees. Will Durant tells us that many physicians were highly specialized. "There were urologists, gynecologists, obstetricians, ophthalmologists, eye and ear specialists, veterinarians, dentists; Romans could have gold teeth, wired teeth, false teeth, bridgework, and plates."

The formulas for many medicines were family secrets. Some, to modern minds, were extremely repulsive. Lizard offal was used as a purgative. Dog excreta was prescribed for angina. The spittle of Vespasian was said to cure blindness, and the touch of his foot was supposed to be good for the lame.

Anesthetics that eliminated pain were unknown; instead, the doctors relied on mandragora juice or atropin. But surgery, although extremely hazardous, was fairly common. Two hundred instruments such as catheters were discovered in the ruins of Pompeii.

Suprisingly, one of the finest books on medicine ever to be published was issued about A.D. 30. Although not a physician, the author, Aurelius Cornelius Celsus, described methods to be used for plastic surgery, tonsillectomy, the removal of cataracts, and even lateral lithotomy—the removal of stones in the bladder.

The horror of germs was unknown to them. Indeed, Galen, a physician who attended gladiators (A.D.130-200), considered pus to be beneficial, and this was not disproved until the time of Pasteur (A.D. 1822-1895)!

If, in spite of what the doctors could do, the patient died, normal Roman funeral procedures followed. After the final breath of the deceased, the nearest relative closed the eyes, adjusted the limbs, and then perhaps placed a coin in the mouth of the corpse. This coin was to pay the fee of the mythical *Charon* whose duty it was to ferry the departed soul across the river *Styx*.

Next, undertakers took charge of the body. If the deceased had been a commoner, it was dressed in a toga. But if the person had held high office, it was suitably robed and crowned with oak or laurel leaves. The leaves on the crown of a rich man might even be fashioned out of gold.

At this point, professional mourners were employed to help the family indicate sufficient grief. A funeral procession was then formed to carry the litter on which the body had been placed. This litter was carried by four men in front and four men behind. The age of the deceased determined the musical instruments used. For a young corpse, flutes were played; for an older one, trumpets were blown.

Having reached the *Forum Romanum*, a eulogy was delivered, the body was placed on a pyre, and a relative lit the flame. Afterwards the ashes were gathered into an urn.

After the ceremonies, a feast was eaten in the tomb where the urn was stored, and nine days later another offering of food was left at the tomb.

The pyre was unknown in Jerusalem, for there the dead were buried in tombs. Also, each procession was led by a woman. Why? "Because," answers a rabbi, "Eve brought death into the world, and therefore a woman should lead death's victims to the grave!"

No worker in New Testament times was displaced by a machine. Automation was unknown. The worker's problem was competition with slaves. During the reign of Augustus a trained vineyard worker could be purchased for 2,000 denarii—or less. And since an owner had merely to clothe, feed, and house his slaves, competition with free labor was keen.

A slave's life could be hard. None was allowed to serve in the army. Augustus, however, had 20,000 slaves chained to the oars in his warships.

Many believed that it was better to have one's work done by slaves than citizens. This was because slaves, as property, could be tortured. Fire, needles, whips, clamps, and other devices had a way of loosening tongues. Occasionally, a slave tried to pass himself off as a citizen or freedman. This was a capital offense and the penalty could be severe. Frequently, the judge's order was quick: *"Pone crucem servo*—place the cross on the slave."

History remembers the words of a slave who was pardoned after being nailed in place. After recovery, he wrote, "On the cross there are only two things: pain and eternity. They tell me I was on the cross twenty-four hours, but I was on the cross longer than the world existed. If there is no time, then every moment is forever" (*Spartacus*, by Howard Fast).

A skilled worker in New Testament times could earn about one denarius (approximately two dollars in 1982 currency) for a dawn to dusk day of work.

A variety of jobs were available. There were brick kilns, bakeries, restaurants, bookstores, the postal system, cement factories, ships, docks to unload, fountains to keep flowing, miles of aqueducts to maintain, chariots to repair, books to copy, roads to build, rents to collect, and mints to operate.

The New Testament world had barbers, lawyers, teachers, doctors, bankers, priests, officials, contractors, and so on. Life in Rome could be hard. But no one starved. There was a dole to provide a minimum living. Also, there were free public baths, libraries, and all sorts of entertainment. In addition, it was popular for men of wealth to bequeath significant sums for citizens of their clienteles.

Other Romans earned their livings from their little farms, gardens, and vineyards. And since the average Roman consumed two quarts of wine each week, grapes were in great demand.

In Jerusalem, the Romans, especially those quartered near the Tower of Antonia, often complained about the smells of burning flesh that oozed out of the Temple. These smells were generated by the many sacrifices that were performed. Curious about the number of lambs that were slaughtered during the Passover season, Nero decreed that they be counted. This was done in A.D. 65, and the number came to 265,000!

But Jerusalem was not the only city in which the smell of sacrificed animals filled the streets. Rome also had its religions which demanded the sacrifice of blood. One of these faiths was *Mithraism*—a faith that came from the East and that taught the resurrection of the body and the immortality of the soul.

The New Testament world was made up of the rich, the very rich, the poor—and slaves. There was a middle class, but when compared to the middle class of our present world, it was very small. In that first century the rich got richer and the poor got poorer. There were several who owned ten thousand slaves— and more. The Roman poet Ovid (43 B.C.—A.D.17?) was a realist when he had a god say, "How little you know the age you live in if you fancy that honey is sweeter than cash in hand!"

On the whole, clothes were homespun and were made out of wool and linen. Cotton was known—it was mentioned as early as 200 B.C.—but it was used mostly for sails and awnings over the windows of the rich. Likewise, silk found its way into the Empire. But it was extremely expensive. "In the third century A.D. three pounds of gold had to be paid for one pound of raw silk dyed purple"(F. R. Cowell, in *Everyday Life in Ancient Rome*). Moreover, its transparency was considered immodest. Many associated it with loose women.

The toga was a badge of Roman citizenship and as the centuries slipped by it tended to become a garment for formal occasions like the tuxedo in our time.

Soldiers, of course, wore helmets; but most of the men were hatless. Women, however, were expected to keep their heads covered. Indeed, there is a record of an aristocratic Roman who got a divorce because his wife appeared in public without her head being covered! Trousers were considered the mark of a barbarian and were taboo for both sexes.

Tunics were popular with both sexes. Those worn by men and boys reached just below the knees, while those used by women dropped to their feet. Safety pins—*fibulae*—were large, clumsy, and popular. Buttons and studs were also used. Normally, however, a simple belt was sufficient to hold a tunic in place.

Wealthy Romans, like wealthy Jews, often had several homes. Fountains, swimming pools, mosaics on the walls and floor, statues, indoor gardens, and wall paintings were popular. The poor had to be content with small, crowded apartments, some located two and three hundred steps up.

The rich had indoor plumbing. The poor had to carry water into their kitchens from nearby springs or wells.

The modest home in which Simon Peter lived probably consisted of several rooms with a flat roof sloped just enough to carry off the rain. There may or may not have been a kitchen. Many Jews preferred to cook outside and during inclement weather, inside a lean-to. The roof provided a fine place to rest in order to get away from it all.

Meals in much of the New Testament world were eaten twice a day. Breakfast—*jentaculum* in Rome—was eaten at sunrise, and generally consisted of the products of wheat: pancakes, rolls, bread. The main meal—*cena*—was enjoyed in mid-afternoon. This meal might consist of vegetables, meat, fish, eggs, fowl, pastries, etc. The Romans served all sorts of birds including ostriches, cranes, and even peacocks. Also, pork was extremely popular. Expensive dinners featured as many as six and seven courses.

Frequently, many hours in the afternoon were spent in

drinking. And since each time the host made the signal the guests were required to empty their cups, there was a lot of drunkeness.

Taxes varied with the times. Often there was a one percent sales tax, custom duties, and a toll for using certain bridges. But Will Durant tells us that the "total annual revenue of the state under Vespasian was at most 1,500,000,000 sesterces ($150,000,000)—less than a fifth of the budget of New York City today." (The dollar figures and New York City taxes are those of 1944!)

In their colonies, the gathering of taxes was left to certain local men. Before Augustus Caesar came to power, taxes were farmed by stock companies in Rome. These companies bid on the amount to be raised in a certain district. Then the highest bidder employed publicans like Matthew and Zacchaeus to ferret out the money. In turn, the publicans raised more than necessary in order to compensate themselves.

There were two classes of publicans: the *gabbai*, and the *mokhsa*. The gabbai collected general taxes: 20 percent of wine and fruit, and 10 percent of all grain. Likewise, they gathered the poll tax. This tax was levied on all men between fourteen years of age and sixty-five; and on all women from twelve years of age to sixty-five. In addition, they gathered a one percent income tax.

The mokhsa were customhouse officials, and they were considered the worst of the lot, for they could stop people and search them for hidden articles.

Matthew was a mokhsa—a customhouse official!

The above outlines the New Testament world in which the message of Christ was flung in the first century. That message, coming from a conquered country, and suspected of being just another form of hated Judaism, seemed doomed. But enlivened by the Holy Spirit, the Word, the resurrected Christ, and regenerated believers, Christ's message took hold. Indeed, by the fifth century, most of the Roman Empire was considered at least *nominally* Christian!

Appendixes

The following information in Appendix 1 is designed to help the reader harmonize people and events in secular history in first century Christianity. It is not in traditional chart form. However, it is felt that this format presents a clarity that will be helpful to you as you study.

RULERS SPANNING NEW TESTAMENT ERA

NAME	RULED	TERMINATION

Julius Caesar   60-44 B.C.   Stabbed

In 46 B.C. Julius Caesar was made dictator. In the previous years of his rule he was one member, with Cneius Pompey and Licinius Crassus of the ruling triumverate of the Roman republic. Crassus was killed fighting the Parthians in 53 B.C., and Pompey and Caesar soon quarreled. Caesar defeated Pompey in 48 and became dictator in 46 B.C.

Herod the Great   37-4 B.C.   Natural death

Julius Caesar had made Herod's father Antipater governor of Palestine in 47 B.C. Antipater made his son Phasael governor of Jerusalem, and son Herod ruler of Galilee. Mark Antony appointed Herod and Phasael as tetrarchs, "rulers of a fourth." It is difficult to determine exactly when Herod came into full power in Palestine, for he acquired power by degrees. However, the Roman Senate declared him "King of the Jews" just prior to 37 B.C.

Augustus Caesar   27 B.C.-A.D.13   Natural death

At Julius Caesar's assassination, Mark Antony, Caius Octavius (Octavian), and Aemilius Lepidus formed the Second Triumvirate. Following a civil war, Octavian and Antony defeated Brutus and Cassius, the assassins of Julius Caesar. Next, Octavian defeated Antony and Cleopatra. In 31 B.C., Octavian was supreme, but he was not voted the title Augustus until 27 B.C., although he had already been ruling for four years.

Herod Archelaus   4 B.C.-A.D. 6   Banished

Upon the death of Herod the Great, Herod Archelaus was made ethnarch—or king—of Judea, Samaria and Idumea. Presumably he was given two sections, or one half of Herod the Great's kingdom, while his brother Antipas and half-brother Philip each received one fourth of the kingdom, according to their father's will. Archelaus is mentioned in

Matthew 2:22. He is known for having rebuilt the royal palace in Jericho. Because of his barbarous and tyrannical treatment of the Jews Augustus Caesar exiled him in Gaul and sent procurators to rule in his place.

Herod Antipas　　　　　*4 B.C.-A.D. 39*　　　　　*Banished*
Upon the death of Herod the Great, his son Herod Antipas was made tetrarch of Galilee and Perea. He put John the Baptist to death; since he happened to be in Jerusalem the night Jesus was tried before Pilate, the latter sent "the Galilean" to Herod, who mocked Him and sent Him back to Pilate. He is mentioned in the New Testament more often than any other Herod. His sordid character reached a new low when he married his niece Herodias, the former wife of his half-brother Philip. He was deposed by the Emperor Caligula and Herodias shared his exile.

Philip the Tetrarch　　　　　*4 B.C.-A.D. 34*　　　　　*Natural death*
In fulfillment of the will of Herod the Great, this son was made tetrarch of Gaulonitis, Trachonitis and Paneas. He is known best for founding the city of Caesarea Philippi, northeast of the Sea of Galilee. At his death his area was assigned to Syria, He has been considered the best of the Herods.

Tiberius Caesar　　　　　*A.D.14-37*　　　　　*Smothered?*
As the son of Augustus' wife Livia, Tiberius was the first of the Julio-Claudian dynasty, which ended with Nero. Known as cunning and cruel, this emperor was in power during the ministry of John the Baptist; the ministry, death and resurrection of Jesus Christ; and the conversion of the apostle Paul. His long and corrupt reign ended in a mysterious death in his seventy-ninth year.

Pontius Pilate　　　　　*A.D. 26-37*　　　　　*Suicide? Beheaded?*
A Roman, Pilate was the fifth procurator of Judea. Formerly part of the kingdom of Archelaus, the province of Judea, including Samaria, was formed when Archelaus was deposed, in A.D. 6. A procurator, as the personal servant of the emperor, was directly responsible to him. Pilate served under Tiberius. His wife Claudia, granddaughter of Augustus and daughter of the third wife of Tiberius, was allowed to accompany him to Judea against custom. A procurator's powers varied according to the terms at the time

of appointment and clearly Pilate was favored by Caesar. Under Pilate's rule, the Jews were allowed considerable self-government. But to inflict the penalty of death, the sentence had to be confirmed by the procurator. According to Tacitus, Christ was put to death when Tiberius was emperor by the procurator Pontius Pilate.

Caligula   *A.D. 37-41*   *Stabbed*

Caligula had royal blood: his paternal grandmother was a daughter of Antony, and his maternal grandmother was the daughter of Augustus. As grandnephew of Tiberius Caesar, he soon was outdoing him in corruptness and is known in history as a tyrant ruler. Declaring himself a god, he attempted to have his statue placed in the Holy of Holies in Jerusalem. On the basis of the friendship they shared from their youth, Herod Agrippa succeeded in persuading him to relinquish his plan. Some of his own bodyguard ended his life with their swords.

Claudius   *A.D. 41-54*   *Poisoned*

An uncle of Caligula and grandnephew of Augustus, Claudius was considered retarded when young. His literary accomplishments however, indicated that he was not the stupid person many thought him to be. During his reign Christians of Rome were expelled from the city, Acts 18:2. After ordering the death of his wife Messalina because of her profligacy, he yielded to the conniving of his niece Agrippina—Caligula's sister—and married her. She succeeded in placing her son Nero on the throne at the death of Claudius. During his reign, Claudius relied heavily on three freedmen, one of which was Pallas, a former slave of his mother Antonia. Thus Pallas helped and shielded his brother Felix in his corruption and misrule as procurator of Judea.

Herod Agrippa I   *A.D. 41-44*   *Natural death*

King Agrippa, grandson of Herod the Great and Mariamne, was first made king of the realm of his uncle, Philip the Tetrarch, now deceased, by Agrippa's friend, Emperor Caligula. Later, because he had helped Claudius in certain matters when he came to the throne, Claudius appointed him king over the entire realm formerly ruled by Herod the Great. He had the apostle James executed, and his own sudden death is described in Acts 12:21-23.

Herod Agrippa II　　　　　　　*A.D. 50-70*　　　　　*Natural death*
Considered by Claudius too young at his father's sudden death to become King of Judea, he was made ruler of Chalcis upon the death of his uncle. In 53 A.D., Nero made him king of Chalcis, as well as areas of Galilee and Transjordan. He is the Herod before whom Paul appeared in Acts 26. As war threatened between Judea and Rome, Agrippa tried to persuade the Jews not to fight; later he fought on the Roman side with Vespasian. Eventually he moved to Rome where he died in A.D. 100.

Felix　　　　　　　　　　*A.D. 52-60?*　　　　*Recalled to Rome*
Antonius Felix was the fourth procurator to rule Judea after the death of Agrippa I. A freedman, formerly—with his brother Pallas—a slave to Antonia, mother of Claudius, he was given the appointment by Claudius. His corruption and misrule apparently was never known by Claudius because of the protection of Pallas, who served in Claudius' government. The account of Paul's appearance before him is found in Acts 23-24. Acts 24:24 speaks of his wife Drusilla being a Jewess. She was his third wife, sister of Agrippa II, and former wife of the King of Emesa. Josephus says he seduced all three wives.

Nero　　　　　　　　　　*A.D. 54-68*　　　　　　*Suicide*
Nero, after his mother Agrippina's evil conniving, ascended the throne of Rome at the age of seventeen, upon the death of his step-father, Claudius. His reign was characterized by a combination of infantile excesses and his maniacal exercise of an iron will. He was the ruler before whom Paul was to appear when he appealed to Caesar (Acts 25:11-12; 26:32; 28:16-31).

Festus　　　　　　　　　　*A.D. ?-62*　　　　　*Died in Office*
Festus came from Rome to take over the office of procurator, or governor, from Felix. Felix was relieved of his duties when his brother Pallas was no longer in favor in the court of Nero. Paul's case was reopened and he appeared before this new governor in Caesarea (Acts 24:27—26:32). Festus wanted Paul tried before the Jews in Jerusalem, but Paul insisted—by his rights as a Roman citizen—on appealing to Caesar. After appearing before Agrippa II, Paul was sent to Rome.

Galba   *A.D. 68*   *Beheaded*
Galba was the next on the throne, but his reign lasted only six months.

Otho   *A.D. 68*   *Suicide*
The Senate made former senator Otho emperor, but the army wanted Vitellius. Otho committed suicide. His reign had lasted only niney-five days.

Vitellius   *A.D. 69*   *Tortured*
The reign of Vitellius lasted less than a year.

Vespasian   *A.D. 70-79*   *Natural death*
Vespasian, who with his son Titus had been fighting the rebel Jews in Palestine, rushed home to Rome to take the throne. Meanwhile, Titus carried on with the battle for Jerusalem. To his dismay, the Jews refused to surrender, and the Temple as well as Jerusalem were virtually destroyed. Titus returned to Rome with his Jewish mistress, Bernice, sister of King Agrippa II. Vespasian began to build the Flavian Amphitheater (The Colosseum), but died at seventy years of age without completing it.

Titus   *A.D. 79-81*   *Natural death*
Titus had been brought up in the courts of Nero as a friend of Nero's son Britannicus. He accompanied Britannicus in his wars in Germany and Britain. He also accompanied his father Vespasian in his campaigns in Palestine and was left there to finish taking Jerusalem when his father returned to Rome to become emperor. After the tragic destruction of Jerusalem, he returned to Rome where he was given a part in the government. At his father's death he became emperor. During his short reign he completed the building of the Colosseum. He died in his forty-second year.

Domitian   *A.D. 81-96*   *Stabbed*
Domitian, younger son of Vespasian, became emperor at the death of his brother Titus. While the reigns of his father and brother were considered relatively good and they were characterized as times of building and improving the empire, Domitian's reign was second only to Nero's in cruelty. He is known as the persecutor of the apostle John and eventually declared himself to be divine. When his wife

Domitia, discovered her name and those of two of his commanders on his list of victims, she planned his death, which was carried out by his own servants. He was denied a public funeral.

Nerva   *A.D. 96-98*   *Natural death*
Nerva, a former praetor and consul, was made emperor by the Senate at the death of Domitian. After Domitian's cruelty, Nerva's mild and constructive rule raised morale in the empire. But his economies cramped the style of some of the officials. The Praetorian Guard demanded that he adopt a proper son to follow him. He adopted Marcus Ulpius Trajanus, and after a reign of only sixteen months, Nerva was replaced by this son, known as Trajan.

Trajan   *A.D. 98-117*   *Natural death*
Trajan was heading an army in Cologne when elected to the throne. He was also known as a "good emperor," being a good administrator and a hard worker. Nevertheless, the persecution of Christians continued under his reign, and among his victims were Ignatius, Bishop of Antioch; and Cleophas, a reputed cousin of Jesus Christ. The Senate was preparing a great welcome for him on his return from conquests in the East, but he died on the way.

Bar-Kokhba   *A.D. 135?*   *Killed*
Inserted here is Simeon Bar-Kokhba, who in A.D.132 made his appearance as a leader of the Jews in their continuing attempts to regain Palestine and hopes to rebuild Jerusalem. Hailed by many as the Messiah, he led the revolting Jews in victories over the Roman army in Palestine. He was declared the President of Israel, made Eleazar the high priest and Akiba leader of the Sanhedrin, and restored animal sacrifices to the worship of the Jews. Jewish Christians rejected his leadership and endured his persecution. In the end, Bar-Kokhba was killed and the site of the city of Jerusalem plowed over by the Romans.

Hadrian   *A.D. 117-138*   *Suicide?*
Hadrian, as Trajan's relative, was made emperor and was the third of what history calls the five good emperors. The other two, who will not be specifically dealt with here, are Antonius Pius and Marcus Aurelius. Hadrian was particularly interested in traveling and construction. He is known for the

Hadrian Wall built across Britain to protect the frontier of Roman Britain from northern invaders. He was involved for years in the Second Revolt of the Jews, and his army under Severus, finally succeeded in crushing the Jewish revolt. He built a new city on the site of Jerusalem and named it Aelia Capitolina.

NOTES TO
THE GENEAOLOGY OF THE HERODS

THE HERODIAN FAMILY AND REFERENCES TO IT
IN THE NEW TESTAMENT

1. Herod the Great (Matthew 2:1-20; Luke 1:5), son of Antipater, governor of Idumea, and grandson of Antipas, an Edomite who was forced by the Jewish high priest and king, John Hyrcanus, to convert to Judaism, founded the Herodian dynasty. Four generations of this family ruled in the Palestinian area during New Testament times. Herod the Great had ten wives and nine sons known to history. His second wife, Mariamne, was a granddaughter of Hyrcanus.

2. After having his two grown sons by Mariamne killed because they had royal blood from their mother and might usurp his throne, Herod made Doris' son Antipater his heir. Eventually Herod had him killed also and made three other sons rulers of various territories in his kingdom.

3. Archelaus, of wife Malthace, was made Ethnarch, King of Judea, and Samaria and Idumea. Scripture mentions him in Matthew 2:22.

4. Philip, of wife Cleopatra, was made Tetrarch of Gaulonitis, Trachonitis and Paneas; he founded the city of Caesarea Philippi. He is mentioned in Luke 3:1. He was the first husband of Herodias' daughter Salome.

5. Herod Philip, of wife Mariamne II, is perhaps best remembered as the first husband of Herodias, daughter of his half-brother Aristobulus and his cousin Bernice. He is the Philip mentioned in Matthew 14:3; Mark 6:17; and Luke 3:19.

6. Herod Antipas, also of wife Malthace, was made Tetrarch of Galilee and Perea. This is the Herod whose name appears the most times in the Bible: the one who put John the Baptist to death, Matthew 14:1-14; Mark 6:14-29; Luke 9:7-9; the one whom Jesus called "that fox," Luke 13:31-33; the one who treated Jesus with contempt and mockingly arrayed Him in a "gorgeous robe" and sent Him again to Pilate, Luke 23:6-12. Other references to this Herod: Mark 8:15; Acts 4:27. He was deposed by the Emperor Caligula.

7. Aristobulus, one of Mariamne I's four sons, married his cousin Bernice, daughter of his father's sister Salome. Their children were, in addition to the notorious Herodias, Agrippa, who became King of Judea, and Herod, King of Chalcis.

8. Herodias, daughter of Aristobulus, married her uncle, Herod Philip; then incurred the denouncement of John the Baptist because she was living with her husband's half-brother, Herod Antipas. She demanded, and got, John's head on a platter, Mark 6:14-29. Her daughter, who danced before Antipas and gave him her mother's request for John's head, is not named in Scripture. Secular history and other sources, however, name her Salome. Her first husband was her great-uncle, Philip the Tetrarch.

9. Herod Agrippa was known as King Agrippa, and is the "Herod, the king," who vexed some of the members of the first century church and killed the apostle James, the brother of John, recorded in Acts 12:1-4. He would have done the same to Peter had not the angel released him from prison, Acts 12:3-11. Herod died suddenly; Acts 12:23 records that he was smitten by an angel and died because he willingly received the people's acclaim as a god and "gave not God the glory."

10. Herod, king of Chalcis, ruled an area in today's southern Lebanon. He married his niece Bernice, daughter of his brother Agrippa.

11. Agrippa II was very young at the time of his father's sudden death, and Judea was ruled by procurators. Five years later, however, Emperor Claudius made him King of Chalcis upon his uncle's death. And later Nero gave him sections of Galilee and Transjordan to rule. His capital was at Tiberius. With his sister Bernice, whose relationship with him was an open scandal, Agrippa II heard the defense of the apostle Paul at the request of Festus, who had recently come from Rome to take over the governorship from Felix, Acts 25:13-27; 26:1-32.

12. Drusilla, sister of Agrippa II, left her husband Azizus, King of Emesa, to marry Antonius Felix, the Roman governor of Judea, Acts 24:24. (The first wife of Felix was also named Drusilla, a granddaughter of Antony and Cleopatra.)

230

Selected Bibliography

To gather material for this book, I made two trips to Israel, Jordan, and Egypt. Also, I drove several thousand miles in Turkey, Italy, and Greece. With notebook and camera, I labored long in order to unearth choice information that would be useful for preachers, Sunday School teachers, lay people, and travelers.

The following books are among those that I found especially useful. Each one is heartily recommended.

Blaiklock, E.M.	*The Zondervan Pictorial Bible Atlas*, 1969.
Cowell, F. R.	*Everyday Life in Ancient Rome*, B. T. Batsford, Ltd. 1961.
Durant, Will	*Caesar and Christ*, Simon and Schuster, 1944.
Elton, Lord	*Gordon of Khartoum*, Alfred A. Knopf, 1954.
Encyclopedia	*Encyclopedia Judaica*, Macmillan, 1972.
Finegan, Jack	*Light From the Ancient Past*, Princeton University Press, 1946; 1959.
Gibbon, Edward	*The Decline and Fall of the Roman Empire*, E. P. Dutton.
Hamblin, Dora Jane, and Crunsfeld, Mary Jane	*The Appian Way. A Journey*, Random House, 1974.
	Interpreter's Dictionary of the Bible, Abingdon, 1962.
Josephus, Flavius	*The Life and Works of Flavius Josephus*, Winston.
Juvenal	*Satire*.
Kenyon, Kathleen M.	*Digging Up Jericho*, Frederick A. Praeger, 1957.
Morton, H. V.	*In the Steps of Paul*, Rich and Cowan, Ltd.
Paoli, Ugo	*Rome—Its People, Life and Customs*, David McCoy, Inc. Longmans Green, 1963.
Perowne, Stewart	*Life and Times of Herod the Great*, Abingdon, 1959.
Pliny the Younger	*Letters*, Loeb Library.
Ramsey, William M.	*St. Paul the Traveller and the Roman Citizen*, Baker Book House.
Sandmel, Samuel	*Herod, Profile of a Tyrant*, Lippincott, 1967.
Suetonius	*The Twelve Caesars*, translated by Robert Graves and published by Penguin Books, 1957.

Tenney, Merrill C. *Pictorial Bible Dictionary*, Zondervan, 1963.

The New Schaff-Herzog Encyclopedia of Religious Knowledge, Baker Book House, 1960.

Wood, J. T.   *Modern Discoveries on the Site of Ancient Ephesus*. The Religious Tract Society, 1890.

Xenophon   *Anabasis*, I. 11 20. The Loeb Classic Library, translated by Carleton L. Brownson.

Yadin, Yigael   *Bar-Kokhba*, Random House, 1971.

Index

Colorful Poster Available

A large, full-color poster titled, "Rulers in the Times of Jesus," is available from the publisher. Suitable for classroom use, ask for RP-2CJ, $2.50. (Add .60, postage and handling.)

Accent Publications
12100 West Sixth Avenue
P. O. Box 15337
Denver, CO 80215